SLICES
OF
AMERICANA

A ROAD TRIP THROUGH AMERICAN
BASEBALL HISTORY

JASON LOVE

SUNBURY PRESS

Mechanicsburg, PA USA

Published by Sunbury Press, Inc.
Mechanicsburg, Pennsylvania

www.sunburypress.com

For information about special discounts for bulk purchases, please contact Sunbury Press Orders Dept. at (855) 338-8359 or orders@sunburypress.com.

To request one of our authors for speaking engagements or book signings, please contact Sunbury Press Publicity Dept. at publicity@sunburypress.com.

FIRST SUNBURY PRESS EDITION: June 2021

Set in Adobe Garamond | Interior design by Crystal Devine | Cover by Lawrence Knorr | Edited by Lawrence Knorr.

Publisher's Cataloging-in-Publication Data
Names: Love, Jason, author.
Title: Slices of americana : a road trip through american baseball history / Jason Love.
Description: First trade paperback edition. | Mechanicsburg, PA : Sunbury Press, 2021.
Summary: With a tankful of gas and a passion for baseball history, Jason Love hits the road to explore historic baseball sites in America, sharing the connections and stories of American baseball passing by. As much as it's an ode to baseball history in America, it's also a tip of the cap to the simple joys, like eating hash browns at a Waffle House.
Identifiers: ISBN 978-1-62006-553-2 (softcover).
Subjects: SPORTS & RECREATION / Baseball / Essays & Writings | SPORTS & RECREATION / Baseball / History | TRAVEL / Special Interest / Sports.

Product of the United States of America
0 1 1 2 3 5 8 13 21 34 55

Continue the Enlightenment!

Dedicated to Sara, Delia, Sophia, and Ian

CONTENTS

PREFACE

Many great books about road trips to different baseball sites have been written over the years. One of my all-time favorites is *Roadside Baseball: The Locations of America's Baseball Landmarks* by Chris Epting. His book takes an in-depth look at historic baseball sites in every state throughout the country. Some of his locations are obvious places to visit, such as Wrigley Field in Chicago. Other locations are a little off the beaten path, such as McCormick Field in Asheville, North Carolina. This is the home ballpark for the minor league Asheville Tourists.

If *Roadside Baseball* is my favorite, *The Soul of Baseball: A Road Trip Through Buck O'Neil's America* by Joe Posnanski is a close second. The author follows Buck O'Neil around the United States as he talks about Negro League baseball, shares stories from his past, and makes a positive connection with every person he meets along the way. O'Neil played baseball for several years and most notably with the Kansas City Monarchs in the 1940s and 1950s. Over the years, O'Neil conducted endless interviews talking about baseball. He never had a negative word to say. O'Neil died in 2006 at 94 years of age.

Baseball in a Grain of Sand: Seeing the Game through a Small Town Season by Bill Gruber is a book I just discovered recently. Gruber's focus is on an American Legion team playing in Moscow, Idaho. This book highlights the joy of baseball in small communities and how it brings people together. These players are not your superstars like Aaron Judge or Justin Verlander. These teams are made up of teenagers still learning the game. *Baseball in a Grain of Sand* is a microcosm which in turn reflects small towns across the United States. He also weaves the history of baseball throughout the narrative of the story.

All three of these books left an impact on me. The book I have written is about my travels involving baseball and the history of the game. The initial concept of my book was to capture different minor league teams throughout the year. The plan changed, though, when COVID-19 crippled travel, sports, the economy, and everyday life. Not just baseball, but life, in general, was put on hold. I used to find comfort in going to a Phillies game with my children. All that went out the window with the "new normal."

This book is made up of seven different chapters. Like a slice of pizza or apple pie, each one can be consumed on its own. But put together each slice completes the pie. The common thread throughout the book is baseball. Although thought of as America's game, the sport evolved over time from the British game of cricket in the 1800s. Just like apple pie most likely came from Dutch immigrants and pizza originated from Naples, Italy, things are often easily defined as American. With that being said, I tried to focus on different aspects of American life through the lens of baseball.

Each chapter also touches upon a certain aspect of America's Pastime. I did not just want to focus on Major League Baseball. I enjoy going to minor league baseball games just as much as watching the Phillies play during the summer. One chapter touches upon Judy Johnson and Negro League Baseball. It is easy to forget how many great Black players played in cities such as Kansas City, Pittsburgh, Birmingham, and Chicago who were not given a chance to play in the MLB until 1947. In other chapters, I write about Little League, Minor League Baseball, some of the forgotten leagues such as the Tobacco State League in North Carolina. Some other subjects of the book include baseball and Father's Day, and the joy of Opening Day. I try mostly to project some positive vibes during these challenging times. The theme throughout the book is that baseball may not be the answer, but it does provide a brief outlet when times are tough.

In addition to baseball, Waffle House was unexpectedly weaved into my story. We ended up stopping at one on most of our trips. Most people see the bold block letters of the restaurant while traveling along a major highway. The popular chain provides hot, simple food at a reasonable cost. Since 1955, Waffle House has served 2.5 billion eggs and 1.8 billion orders of hash browns. Their cooks are kept busy. The restaurant also has a place in popular culture. Kid Rock once started a brawl in a DeKalb County, Georgia Waffle House in 2007. Rock landed in jail for 12 hours and eventually settled out of court. During the coronavirus pandemic, many of the restaurants had to close temporarily. One knows things are bad when even the local Waffle House is forced to shut down.

Despite everything happening, there were signs of hope. People stepped forward to help one another. We became used to wearing face coverings when going into the grocery store. Although we could not go to the movies, theater, or sporting events, families learned how to spend time with one another again. We shall overcome these hardships. Will life ever return to how it once was before this pandemic? It is too hard to say. However, a person can find signs of hope in small, everyday moments. My book tries to highlight some of the good moments.

ACKNOWLEDGMENTS

Thank you to Sunbury Press for giving me the opportunity to share my love of baseball.

INTRODUCTION

It was the worst of times. It was the absolute worst of times.

There was a disconnect. In life, the lines are often blurred. It is not always easy to find one's sense of purpose. I would often beat myself up over trying to find what I was supposed to do in life. I have a good job, physical health, three healthy children who are smart, funny, and independent. Yet, I still sometimes find myself at a loss. I feel like Charlie Brown as he lines up to kick the football right before Lucy pulls it away.

A few years ago, I was overcome with a depression that was a real punch to the gut. I have always leaned towards seeing the negative rather than the positive in life. However, this depression was different. I could not explain it. The less I could figure out why the more it drove me into a panic. To this day, I am still not sure why I was in such a funk. Someone told me about having an allergic reaction to a medicine I took for an illness. Somehow one of the side effects attacked my nervous system. I am not sure. It was just a horrible feeling. It was very humbling as well. I now have deep empathy for people dealing with depression.

It was through baseball that I found some relief. After coming home from work, I would have a catch with my son Ian. The rhythm of catching the baseball, throwing it, making small talk with my son, and then repeating the motions brought comfort. It sounds too simple, but it helped to quiet my thoughts. Having a catch was like mindful breathing in a way—a Zen-like moment involving a baseball and a mitt. Not to sound like James Earl Jones in *Field of Dreams*, but baseball has been the one consistent comfort in my life.

After having a baseball catch or taking my children to see the Phillies play, I started to understand the power of sports fully. There is a connection between people tailgating for hours before a football game in a parking lot. It could be a mother and a daughter traveling to Chattanooga, Tennessee, for a softball tournament. It may be two strangers sitting at some blue-collar bar watching a game on television. They share in the moment of Michael Jordan throwing down a dunk or Mario Lemieux finessing a puck past a goalie.

Even sports like running or golfing seem to be more enjoyable when done with other people. I could never understand why people sign up for a 5K race. Don't they get the same workout from running alone in the streets? Running a race with other people is about the connection and the shared experience. A person who golfs with three other friends on a Saturday afternoon can share in the joy of hitting the ball onto the green. Baseball is the same way.

At seven years old, I started playing Little League baseball in South Jersey. A baseball league for kids was not as organized or polished in the early 1980s as it is today. Children playing sports did not have to do indoor training, play all year round, or have personal trainers. I am not exactly sure how this evolved over the years. My love of baseball began with Little League and with watching the Phillies. My father did not take me to many games when I was a kid. He liked sports, but for whatever reason, he did not like going to games. He did not like dealing with traffic. Despite his indifference to going to see games in person, I was drawn to sports. I especially liked baseball.

Truth be told, I was an average player (and even that may be an exaggeration). I just loved playing, hanging out at the snack stand, and the camaraderie of my teammates. One of my finest moments was playing third base when I was around nine years old. This heavyset kid hit a bullet down the third baseline. I somehow stopped it with my head. I staggered a bit, picked up the ball, and threw it over to first base. The umpire called the hitter out. It was a nice play. I think it helped that the kid was probably one of the slowest runners in the league.

Some of my earliest memories are of the 1980 World Series with Pete Rose, Tug McGraw, and Mike Schmidt. I remember watching *This Week in Baseball* on Saturday mornings. Sometimes after a few beers, I will play the opening on YouTube just to hear Mel Allen's voice. I also remember watching *The Baseball Bunch* with Johnny Bench and the Famous Chicken. I thought how lucky the kids were on that show. Like a lot of kids in the 1980s, I collected baseball cards. I kept a bunch of them, but they are not worth much money. I still look at my old cards now and then bring back childhood memories when I need a lift. I have a Steve Jeltz signed card. He played shortstop for the Phillies and retired with a .210 batting average. That is about what my batting average was when I quit playing baseball.

When my daughter Delia was just a toddler, I started taking her to games at Veterans Stadium. I wanted to share my love of sports with all three of my children. I have a photo of me holding little Delia next to the Phillie Phanatic in the 700-level of The Vet. She is probably one year old. She has this look on her face like she is not sure what to make of this giant, furry mascot. It's a great memory. When I am feeling down in the dumps, I look at old photos of my children at different ball games. Just like the old baseball cards, the photos always seem to lift my spirits.

Through the winter of 2019, I found myself staring at a few long, cold months (it was a rather mild winter, but that does not sound as good). During the previous summer, my wife Sara and I agreed that divorce was probably for the best. We had met in college at West Chester University. She is a good person, a great mom to our three children, and a hard-working nurse. I cannot say anything bad about her. But, we just stopped getting along. Her family never warmed up to me. My wife's father did not even show at our wedding. I think he was watching a Three Stooges marathon on television that day instead. At first, it bothered me, but eventually, I did not care. My wife and her family are from Upper Darby in Delaware County, Pennsylvania ("Delco" is what most people call it). I started to think people from Delco, and South Jersey just aren't meant for one another. We are both too stubborn and set in our ways. About the only thing we can agree upon is our unabashed love for Wawa (for those readers not familiar with it, Wawa is a convenience store that people in Pennsylvania/New Jersey frequent at least once a day). Wawa is like 7-Eleven but only better.

In July 2019, I moved back into the house I grew up in. My mother passed away on February 13, 2018, so it was just my dad living there. He welcomed me back. We have always gotten along. It was weird, though, moving back into my childhood home. It was especially weird with my mom not being around. Sometimes I can still hear her voice telling me to tuck in my shirt or stand up straight. It's a strange feeling moving into your old house while your own three kids live in another house about a mile away. On the other hand, my wife and I seem to get along better now that we have separated. Go figure.

In my old bedroom, I found some photos of my Little League team. Our team looked like it stepped out of a scene from *The Bad News Bears* with Mr. Buttermaker. I also found some of my old baseball cards. I remember how the 1985 Dwight Gooden card was gold for a 12-year-old kid. I also found some of my old Sports Illustrated magazines, including the famous swimsuit issues. I remember how Elle Macpherson was considered the gold standard for a 12-year-old kid in the 1980s. She still looks amazing today. There must be something said for regular exercise and drinking plenty of water.

I remember one specific SI issue where Wade Boggs, Don Mattingly, and Ted Williams talked about the art of hitting. Baseball has a way of making connections across generations. A father can talk about Mickey Mantle being the greatest Yankee while the son likes Derek Jeter. It has been special for me to take my daughters and son to baseball games over the years. Sometimes going to the ballpark is not even about watching a baseball game. Baseball is the best sport for allowing conversation throughout the game. There is always a pause between pitches or a few minutes between innings.

When I was in my early twenties, I had visions of being the next Charles Bukowski, Ernest Hemingway, or John Fante. As a writer living alone in an apartment, I saw myself smoking cigarettes, drinking cheap beer, and typing away on my typewriter. It would be a solitary existence. I would write the next *Old Man and the Sea*. Life did not exactly turn out that way. My path took a different turn, but I have no complaints. My oldest daughter Delia was born while I was in my mid-20's. Sophia followed four years later. Ian was born in 2007. Reflecting on the misguided dreams of my youth, I cannot imagine a life without having children. All three of my kids bring me such joy. I am sure most parents feel the same way. I would be lost without my two daughters and son.

There is a cliché about life that the only thing constant is change. With my marriage ending and my children getting older, I felt life again was heading in a different direction. Or maybe I had no direction. It's hard to say. I hear the song *Landslide* by Fleetwood Mac and think, "that's me in a nutshell." So the idea came to visit baseball sites with the hope of giving me some type of direction. Or maybe it was a connection with my children. Maybe it was more about the journey itself rather than a specific destination.

The road trips for this book are only the beginning. Traveling to places like Baltimore, Cooperstown, Williamstown, Pennsylvania, and North Carolina are just the tip of the iceberg. Once things settle down, I would like to visit Dodger Stadium, check out the Negro League Baseball Museum in Kansas City, catch a few Spring Training games in Florida and maybe even try a Rocky Mountain Po'Boy (Google it) at Coors Field. Life is short. Or at least that is what I have heard. How can I call myself a baseball fan if I have never been to Wrigley Field?

The book's overall theme crept in my head when I realized that baseball, Babe Ruth, *Bull Durham*, Cooperstown, the open road, and even Waffle House represents what is good about the United States. Baseball has a way of uniting people regardless of race, religion, economic background, social status, or whatever else people use to label a human being. Although Ruth's career finished before Jackie Robinson broke the color barrier in 1947, his barnstorming trips took him to all corners of the country. Ruth was beloved by both Black and white baseball fans. Heck, the Babe even traveled to places such as Hawaii and Japan to share his love of baseball. He came from a rough and tumble upbringing to become the world's first superstar.

And is there anything more American than a Waffle House? Founded by Joe Rogers Sr. and Tom Forkner in 1955, this restaurant chain serves hot, rather simple meals that keeps people coming back. What started in Georgia, the restaurant now has locations primarily in the South but now stretches into Oklahoma, New Mexico, and Texas. The block, yellow lettering, is a welcome site for many weary travelers on the highway. Whether you pull up in a BMW, motorcycle, or a Ford F-100 pickup truck from the 1970s, anyone can enjoy an inexpensive meal at the Waffle House. As we visited the different sites, the Waffle House kept popping up along the way. How could I write a travel book without touching upon this classic restaurant? Even Anthony Bourdain had a soft spot in his heart for this iconic waffle chain.

The plan was simple, but then the world quickly went south. I would visit a few baseball sites with my children, eat at Waffle Houses and write about our observations. Then, with the arrival of spring, I was going to incorporate my love of baseball with the joys of traveling, talking with people, and creating new memories. It seemed simple enough. What could possibly go wrong?

This book is unexpectedly divided into two parts. When the COVID-19 pandemic struck the entire world, it was unlike any other type of disaster. For myself and so many others, it was difficult to grasp the magnitude of the situation. I have always had good physical health, but I became afraid of getting the virus and passing it along to someone more vulnerable. The Earth's rotation seemed to come to a halt. Hundreds of Waffle Houses even had to close during the shutdown of our country. After weeks of working from home, not going to restaurants or sporting events, all I wanted to do was travel once it became safe. Americans seem to have the traveling bug in our bloodstream. Whether we are going on vacation, out to eat, or driving across the country. We do not like to stay in one place for too long. The United States is a country of constant motion.

During the summer of 2019, my son and I visited four of the five minor league ballparks in New Jersey. I wanted to visit all five, but we ran out of time to visit the New Jersey Jackals at Montclair State University. However, we did visit the Trenton Thunder, Lakewood BlueClaws, Somerset Patriots, and the Sussex County Miners. Ian received baseballs from players at both Lakewood and Sussex County. The trips were a lot of fun, and each ballpark had a unique aspect to it. I wrote a short book about the experience and self-published it. The experience gave me the idea to explore the idea of expanding our trips outside the Garden State.

I am not sure this book will provide any answers. I am not even sure of the questions. Who writes a book about visiting different baseball sites when sports were essentially placed on hold? If anything, the shutdown of 2020 made me realize how much I missed sharing the sports experience with my friends and family. I no longer care as much about the outcome of games, or wins and losses, or even if my team wins the championship. I have come to realize there are so many more important aspects to life. However, going to the ballpark with my son is something I look forward to each year. If anything, baseball provides the backdrop and allows us to talk about life.

Steve Jobs gave his famous commencement speech at Stanford University in 2005. He spoke about dropping out of Reed College as a young man. Since he no longer had an exact plan of study, he decided to take a calligraphy class. While taking this class, he learned to appreciate different brush strokes, fonts, and things like that. It was not part of any plan at the time. However, years later, when he started Apple, he realized he could use the knowledge from his calligraphy class into the different fonts for personal computers. Jobs looked back at his life during Reed College and connected the dots. This book is my attempt to connect the dots while also looking at the future.

Hopefully, this short book captures the baseball road trips my children Delia, Sophia and Ian, and I took to different baseball sites throughout the country. In the spirit of *Travels with Charley* or *On the Road*, I wanted to take some road trips to find the missing piece. What is the missing piece? I have a hard time explaining. It is sort of like something that gnaws at you in the middle of the night. When everyone in a room is laughing at some joke, you find yourself wondering what is so funny. It is waiting out the Coronavirus with the rest of the nation but secretly itching to be on the road.

As a child, my family and I would take a few road trips for vacations. We visited Bar Harbor, Maine, and Cape Cod. We went to Walt

Disney World. My mother worked as a travel agent and then eventually owned her own agency. We visited a few far-off places like Jamaica and the Grand Canyon. Once I became a teenager, though, I didn't want to go on vacation. I'm not sure why, except I was a stubborn teenager. So I missed out on some fun trips.

For the most part, my life has been simply striving to show up at work, pay my bills, keep a roof over my head and provide for my children. It has not been an adventurous life by any means. My life is boring for the most part. I am just a normal (hopefully people think so) guy trying to make his way in the world. I love baseball, meeting new people, visiting new places, and spending time with my family. I hope you enjoy the book, and it inspires you to set off on your own adventures.

BABE RUTH

DECEMBER 26–27, 2019

"Who goes to Baltimore in December?"

For our first baseball-related visit, I chose the Babe Ruth Birthplace and Museum. Baltimore is relatively close to my home. It is only about a two-hour drive from New Jersey. My children Delia, Sophia, Ian, and I decided to travel south on I-95 over the Christmas holiday. Most people probably think Key West or Aruba to escape the winter blues, but Baltimore is what I could afford at the time. My son and I have visited numerous baseball sites in the last few years. I usually drag him along with me when I want to see some historic baseball site. Luckily, Ian is a good sport about seeing a gravesite of some old player, a minor league ballpark in need of repair, or a mural of Jackie Robinson in North Philadelphia.

George Herman Ruth was born in the Pigtown section of Baltimore in 1895. Ruth did not receive the nickname "Babe" until much later when he started playing baseball for the Orioles. Around the time he was born, pigs were unloaded from the Baltimore & Ohio Railroad trains. This area was known for its numerous butcher shops. Ruth's birthplace and the museum itself are located just a stone's throw away from Camden Yards. His father's saloon was in the approximate location of the ballpark's centerfield.

At the age of seven, a young Ruth was sent by his parents to St. Mary's Industrial School for Boys. Ruth was deemed "incorrigible" and would spend the rest of his childhood there. With his father running the business, the young Ruth had little supervision growing up. He threw rocks at people, chewed tobacco, and refused to go to school. Ruth's mother died when he was 12 years old. Ruth would later say that while at St. Mary's that his parents never visited him. Ruth's childhood almost seems to be something out of a Charles Dickens' novel.

Ruth's parents divorced while he was quite young. Many of his siblings died early in their childhood. It is believed that alcohol paid a big part in the divorce. There is also the rumor that Ruth's mother was unfaithful. Ruth had one sister who lived to adulthood. Mary Margaret "Mamie" Ruth was the Babe's younger sister. Mamie lived in Baltimore for most of her life until her later years when she moved to Hagerstown, Maryland. She passed away in 1992 at 91 years of age. Neither Mamie nor Babe said much about their childhood. Mamie was protective though of her older brother's legacy. If you look at photos of her, she has a strong resemblance to the Babe. One can only imagine it was a troublesome childhood as the family moved around quite a bit before settling above their father's saloon. Mamie was just a toddler when her older brother was sent away to live at St. Mary's.

It was while at St. Mary's that Ruth picked up the game of baseball. Brother Matthias taught Ruth the game. He was a large man and made a strong connection to the young Ruth. Matthias became the father figure that Ruth lacked in his life. His time spent at St. Mary's instilled in the future slugger a love for children and a soft spot in his heart for the downtrodden. Despite his wealth and fame through baseball, the Babe always took time out for the less fortunate.

It seems from different reports that the young Ruth was often teased about his looks. He was often called names that I prefer not to use for this book. Children did not spend the bulk of their childhood at St. Mary's. Ruth was an exception. Toward the end of his stint, he was by far the largest child living there. He would finally leave after getting noticed by the Baltimore Orioles in 1914. This was not the Orioles we know today. The Orioles would eventually sell the talented young Ruth to the Boston Red Sox, where his career took off. Ruth started as a dominant pitcher. He didn't become the prolific home run hitter until he moved on to the New York Yankees.

With all due respect to Willie Mays, Hank Aaron, and Ty Cobb, Babe Ruth was the greatest baseball player of all time. Jackie Robinson must be given credit for all that he did in 1947 when he took the field for the Brooklyn Dodgers. I am always amazed at the courage of Robinson and for what he went through in the 1940s and 1950s. His baseball stats, however, do not match that of Ruth. When you look at his home runs, his connection with the fans, and his impact on the game, it is hard to argue against Ruth. He was truly the first superstar of baseball and helped save the game after the 1919 Black Sox scandal.

I am not sure what I was hoping to accomplish by visiting Baltimore during the Christmas holiday of 2019. Since my kids were off from school, I wanted to get away and spend some time with them. My wife and I were together for more than 20 years. I knew Christmas was going to be difficult. I thought a visit to Baltimore and a walk around the Inner Harbor would take our minds off the impending divorce and separation.

My knowledge of Baltimore is limited to Edgar Allan Poe, *Hairspray*, the aquarium, and the television show *The Wire*. I remember the Baltimore Orioles beat the Phillies in the 1983 World Series. I think of the Orioles, and Cal Ripken, Jr. is the player who comes to mind. Anthony Bourdain visited Baltimore for one of his television shows. It looked like a cool place to visit. Bourdain ate a restaurant with Snoop from *The Wire*. It seems like a gritty, blue-collar city with an eclectic restaurant scene. One of the greatest television characters of all time is Omar from *The Wire*. He is not your typical villain.

Baltimore has a special connection to South Jersey as well. Joe Flacco grew up in Audubon, New Jersey, which is not far from my hometown. He was drafted out of the University of Delaware by the Ravens in the 2008 NFL Draft. Flacco helped the Ravens win the Super Bowl for the 2012 season. He is still the pride of South Jersey when it comes to football. If you drive through Audubon, a few Ravens flags still hang from the front porches of homes.

Another Baltimore native and almost as famous as Babe Ruth is H.L. Mencken. He was known as the "Sage of Baltimore" and a prolific writer in the early 20th Century. Mencken lived his entire life in Charm City (1524 Hollins Street) and was known for such quotes as "no one ever went broke underestimating the taste of the American public." Mencken, *The Wire,* and Cal Ripken, Jr.? What's not to like about Baltimore? It seemed like the perfect place for a guy like Babe Ruth to grow up in. My kids just like to get away. When they were younger, all three loved staying in hotels. As long as a hotel had an indoor pool, an elevator, an ice machine, and a free breakfast, my kids were in heaven. So we set out on the morning of December 26, 2019, in my daughter's Toyota Corolla. Unfortunately, my Dodge Journey was with a mechanic because the check engine light was on. My last three vehicles have been Dodges, and I have always had issues. Some people never learn.

Baltimore is south of the Mason-Dixon Line. It has a different feel than Philadelphia, New York, and Boston. Maryland was a slave state due to its tobacco industry; however, Baltimore had a large population of freed slaves. At one time, the city was the second-largest port of entry for immigrants trailing only New York City. Neighborhoods such as Greektown and Little Lithuania reflect the diverse nature of Baltimore.

"Can I get a waffle?"

Before heading to Baltimore, though, we had to make a stop along I-95. My kids wanted to stop at a Waffle House for breakfast. For reasons unknown, my daughter Sophia and son Ian really like Waffle House. I don't know of any that exist in New Jersey. We ate there a few times when on vacation in Florida a few years ago. Maybe it is something from eating at the Waffle House in St. Petersburg, Florida, that triggers pleasant memories for Sophia. Since we pass one on the way to Maryland, it was agreed upon to stop for breakfast at the Waffle House in Elkton, Maryland.

For those not familiar with Waffle House, it is a semi-fast food restaurant that is known mostly for its breakfast foods and iconic yellow lettering. Most Waffle Houses are along major interstates, or near rest stops. The restaurant was founded in 1955, and there are about 1,500 scattered across the United States, primarily in the South. The farthest one north that I am aware of is in Clark's Summit in Pennsylvania. The simple, yellow block lettering sign can be spotted from most major interstates.

We pulled off I-95 and stopped at the Waffle House in Elkton. This town in Maryland was the place to go for young married couples from Pennsylvania, Delaware, and New Jersey to elope. Right over the Delaware-Maryland border, couples would stop in Elkton to get married without the wait. I am not sure if this is still the case. Until the 1930s, Maryland did not have a waiting period for people to apply for a marriage license.

My 12-yeard old son is a vegan, so basically, the only thing he could get from the menu was hash browns. I like the simplicity of this chain restaurant. Waffle House is a very "what you see is what you get" type of restaurant. Our server was very friendly, the food was cheap, and the coffee was hot. Sometimes it's the little things in life are what's important. I ordered eggs, biscuits, and some grits. Delia and Sophia ordered waffles. Ian settled for hash browns with onions.

One thing I learned about Waffle House is that FEMA determines the severity of a disaster on whether the restaurant stays open. The FEMA Waffle House index is coded in green, yellow, and red. Green means the restaurant is fully open with all its menu options. Yellow means it is open but has a limited menu which could be for different reasons. Red is the worst and indicates the restaurant is closed until further notice. When we visited, the FEMA index must have been green because they offered the full menu. The place was packed with people. During this time, the coronavirus was just a whisper but nothing more.

Waffle House, like the game of baseball, has its own quirky lingo. Baseball uses phrases such as a "Texas Leaguer" for a bloop single or "can of corn" for a routine fly ball to the outfield. At a Waffle House, one can order hash browns several different ways at the restaurant chain. Smothered is with sautéed onions. Chunked is with cut-up pieces of ham. Capped is with mushrooms. Country is with a sausage gravy poured on top. Ian ordered his "scattered," which is simply spread on the grill to get the potatoes a little crispy. After we finished our meal, we were back on the road.

Since not many people are itching to visit Baltimore in the dead of winter, I was able to book a room at the Hyatt Regency near the Inner Harbor for a reasonable price. I chose this hotel since I could park the car and then not worry about driving around the city. Unfortunately, as a creature of the suburbs, my parallel parking skills in cities are subpar. Along with the Babe Ruth Museum, we wanted to check out the National Aquarium in Baltimore. Since Chesapeake Bay is known for its crabs, I also wanted to get a sandwich somewhere in the city. I settled for a crab cake sandwich at Tir na nOg, an Irish pub chain restaurant. Not exactly authentic crab cake, but it was decent. The crab meat was probably cod fish with old bay seasoning.

Our room had a great view of the harbor. We could see the aquarium, the various chain restaurants, and Ripley's Believe It or Not Odditorium. In the distance, I could see the Domino Sugars sign. The sugar factory is still in operation in Baltimore and employs more than 500 people. I love history and learned Domino has been going strong in Baltimore for more than 90 years. The location processes more than six million pounds of raw sugar per day. The sign itself is about 70' by 120' and illuminated by 650 glass tubes. It gives off a reddish-orange flow when lit. When I put some Domino sugar in my coffee now, I will have more of an appreciation of the process behind it.

We arrived in Baltimore around noon. We parked the car, but it was too early to check-in. I figured we could walk the few blocks to the Babe

Ruth Museum. I should have planned out the directions better, but I thought we could just follow Delia's iPhone. What should have been a 10-minute walk took us over an hour. Her phone kept recalibrating our location, so we walked in a circle about three or four times.

"Look, kids! Big Ben! Parliament!"

The joke did not go over too well. My kids are not fans of Chevy Chase.

After walking around Little Italy for half an hour and then back to the Inner Harbor, we finally started heading in the right direction. Baltimore is a very walkable city made up of about 250 different neighborhoods. For a December afternoon, the weather was perfect. I finally broke down and asked a police officer for the direction for the ballpark. By this time, though, we were about one block away. He kind of just pointed and said, "right there."

The home of the Baltimore Orioles became the blueprint for all the MLB ballparks built within the last 25 years. Camden Yards was a dramatic shift away from the multi-purpose stadiums that became popular during the early 1970s. I grew up going to Veterans Stadium in South Philadelphia to watch the Phillies. The Vet fell right in line with these "cookie-cutter" stadiums such as Three Rivers Stadium and Shea Stadium. Baltimore did something different. Ruth was born just a few short blocks from the outfield of Camden Yards. This neighborhood has plenty of restaurants and bars within walking distance of the ballpark. Although the Orioles are not a great team, Camden Yards is still a nice ballpark to visit.

The Orioles have a bit of connection to most Phillies fans. As I mentioned, the Baltimore team featuring Cal Ripken, Jr., Eddie Murray, Jim Palmer, and Rick Dempsey defeated Philadelphia in the 1983 World Series. This was referred to as "The I-95 Series" since the teams only had to travel about two hours up or down the interstate to play their away games. During the World Series, neither team traveled by plane since the cities are so close. The Phillies team featured former Reds players Joe Morgan, Tony Perez, and Pete Rose. The Orioles won in five games. Although only in his second full season in Major League Baseball, this was Ripken's only World Series appearance in his long career.

Baltimore may be the birthplace of Babe Ruth, but Maryland is Cal Ripken, Jr. all the way. He is admired for the 2,632 game-streak and Hall of Fame career, but his presence is still felt throughout the state. After he retired, Ripken purchased a minor league team in 2002 and relocated it to Aberdeen, Maryland. The team was renamed the IronBirds and is now an affiliate of the Orioles. His business ventures also include youth baseball tournaments called The Ripken Experience. These popular tournaments have locations in Aberdeen, Pigeon Forge, Myrtle Beach, and Orlando. Each location features numerous ballfields, batting cages, camps, and even hotels. Kids love it as they feel like they are part of a professional team. Ripken has proven to be just as successful running his minor league team and the youth baseball games.

Cal Ripken, Jr. is still the face of the Baltimore Orioles. The kids and I roamed around Camden Yards and took a few photos in the outdoor picnic area. It was open to the public, and I was able to get some nice shots. The Orioles have a few statues of legendary Orioles players. There is a statue of Babe Ruth as well. Ruth played briefly for the Orioles (at the time, a minor league team). The statue is named "Babe's Dream" and is of a younger Ruth and not the more robust-looking player of the New York Yankees. The Orioles manager Jack Dunn learned about Ruth's baseball skills at St. Mary's. In the middle of the 1914 season, the Orioles shipped Ruth to the Boston Red Sox along with two other players for cash.

It was kind of confusing to find the Babe Ruth Birthplace & Museum. I thought there would be more signs pointing the way. Finally, we noticed on the ground are painted baseballs which sort of lead the way. They are painted about every 10 feet or so. The museum is located near the outfield area of Camden Yards across the street on Emory Street. The historic home opened to the public in 1974 after years of falling into disrepair. The Babe Ruth Birthplace & Museum is now run by a non-profit foundation and attracts thousands of visitors each year. The crowds tend to be larger when the Orioles are playing and fans are visiting the ballpark.

Camden Yards is still a great place to see a ballgame. My first game at the ballpark was on June 17, 2000 (I saved the ticket stub: Section 316, Row KK, Seat 7 for $18.00). I cannot remember much of the game except that Mo Vaughn was playing for the Anaheim Angels. Vaughn hit a home run in the 8th inning. I always liked him as a player. The Orioles team had Ripken (of course), Albert Belle, Will Clark, and Harold Baines. It was Ripken's second to last year as a player. The Orioles won only 74 games that year. Camden Yards has a great atmosphere. I remember getting a grilled sausage on a roll with pepper and onions. Despite a horrible Orioles team, the atmosphere was festive in the outdoor area of Eutaw Street. Baltimore's fans showed a lot of pride in their team. Although the Orioles have not fielded a good team in quite a few years, the ballpark is still a wonderful place to visit.

The museum is the location where Ruth was born on February 6, 1895. It was the home of his maternal grandfather. The street is lined with neat brick rowhomes. As we entered the home, it was like taking a step back in time. There is a small gift shop inside where visitors pay the $10 admission fee. My children didn't quite fully appreciate the history of Babe Ruth. However, my son Ian who plays Little League baseball, was interested in some of the baseball artifacts.

On the ground floor is a small exhibition space where a film showed the significance of the *Star-Spangled Banner*. The national anthem has a special connection to Baltimore. The anthem comes from a poem written by Francis Scott Key, who penned it after the British attack on Fort McHenry in Baltimore Harbor during the War of 1812. Key was inspired by watching the United States flag fly while the British ships bombed the fort. Major League Baseball started playing the *Star-Spangled Banner* at ball games during WW I. The fans seemed to enjoy it, and it raised their patriotism for the country during those turbulent times.

The Babe Ruth Birthplace and Museum has numerous artifacts, uniforms, baseball bats, and photos related to the legendary slugger. It is incredible the heaviness of the bat Ruth used in the early part of his career. According to the legend, he used bats weighing between 40 to 54 ounces. He later switched to a lighter bat. Just as a comparison, most current Major League players use a bat weighing around 32 ounces. When it comes to Babe Ruth, his legend and the facts often become too blurred to grasp the actual truth fully.

The museum housed different uniforms worn by Ruth. Another interesting fact is that he never wore the Yankees uniform with the interlocking NY on the jersey. The Yankees did not introduce this logo on their jerseys until 1936. The museum also had some great photos of Ruth standing next to Lou Gehrig. Ruth and Gehrig playing on the same team is incredible. The lineups of some of these Yankees teams did not have much of a weakness.

Some numbers just resonate in baseball. People associate number 42 with Jackie Robinson. Joe DiMaggio is linked with his 56-game hitting streak. Babe Ruth and 714 home runs are connected forever. Although Hank Aaron and Barry Bonds would eventually surpass Ruth, the number 714 is synonymous with the home run. Ask a casual baseball fan how many home runs Bonds ended up with, and he or she cannot probably come up with the number.

Frank "Home Run" Baker was the premier slugger before Babe Ruth came along. He played primarily with the Philadelphia Athletics and was the league leader in home runs with 12 in 1913. Baker retired after the 1922 season with 93 home runs. One cannot compare different eras in baseball, but Chris Sabo, who primarily played in the 1990s with the Cincinnati Reds, retired with 116 home runs. Then, Babe Ruth came along and basically changed the entire approach to hitting the baseball. He signaled the end of the "Deadball Era" of baseball.

In 1919 Ruth began his transition from pitcher to an everyday player and hit 29 home runs to lead Major League Baseball. Second was Gavvy Cravath of the Phillies with 12 home runs. In his debut with the Yankees in 1920, Ruth hit an incredible 54 home runs. That was more than most teams hit collectively that season. With his mighty swing, Ruth made every at-bat a must-watch moment for the fans. And despite swinging for the fences, he still retired with a .342 lifetime batting average. Over 22 seasons, Ruth struck out a total of 1,330 times. Chris Davis of the Orioles has already struck out 1,835 through the 2019 season. Ruth's numbers still hold up over time.

The Babe played the bulk of his career during the Prohibition era. For a player to enjoy a beer now and then, alcohol was banned in the

United States from 1920 to 1933. Ruth enjoyed booze, women, and the nightlife; however, he put up incredible numbers year after year. Only in 1925 were his numbers affected by his exuberant lifestyle. Unfortunately, Ruth was ill that year (the true reason was never officially known) and played in only 98 games. He bounced back, though, in 1926 and hit 47 home runs while batting .372 for the season. From 1926 through 1931, Ruth led the American League in home runs. However, he was more than a home run hitter as he batted .393 in 1923 and .378 in 1924. In 1923 Ruth also earned an incredible 170 walks to go with 205 hits.

It is a shame the steroid era warped the home run totals of the players. In reflection, the Sammy Sosa-Mark McGwire bromance was nothing but a fraud. Alex Rodriguez and his 696 home runs are tainted by his use of performance-enhancing drugs. The top three home runs hitters of baseball are forever Hank Aaron, Babe Ruth, and Willie Mays. If Mays did not miss the 1953 season due to military service, he most likely would have reached 700 home runs. Aaron was a consistently great home run hitter. Bud Selig's biggest mistake was how little he regarded the all-time statistics of baseball. The history books are forever ruined by players who went around the rules to achieve their glory. But the game lives on.

There were a few other visitors at the museum on the day we went there. Amazingly, 100 years after that, Ruth was sold by the Boston Red Sox that his legend still lives on one hundred years later. No other player had the impact on the game as Ruth. Even my children enjoyed the museum. It is tough to separate fact from fiction when it comes to the Babe. Did he really call his shot against the Cubs in the World Series? Did Ruth promise to hit a home run for a sick kid and then came through? Did he eat nothing but hot dogs, drink beer, yet still play at such an elite level? Ruth seemed to do it all. He did not just hit monster home runs, but Ruth connected with the fans like no other player since.

Baseball needs a personality like Ruth's in today's game. The superstars of the sport, such as Mike Trout, Mookie Betts, Clayton Kershaw, Jose Altuve, and even Bryce Harper, do not have the same advertising pull as Lebron James, Tom Brady, or even Zion Williamson. I give pitcher Trevor Bauer credit. He voices his opinions and is active on social media. Bauer is not one of the elite players in baseball, though. Today's players do not have much in terms of personality. Can you imagine if Ruth played in today's game with Instagram and Twitter?

Although he began his career with the Boston Red Sox, I always think of Babe Ruth as a New York Yankee. It is hard to believe that he finished with the Boston Braves in the National League in 1935. His last game was against the Phillies at the Baker Bowl. He was out of shape and a shell of himself. It bothers me that he finished his career with the Braves. I am not sure why. When I was in kindergarten, a friend told me Santa Claus was not real. I shrugged my shoulders and accepted it. The story of sliding down a chimney was a bit far-fetched. Ruth retired with the Boston Braves in 1935. All things considered, I should probably just shrug it off. It is easier to get through life that way.

After we left the museum, we stopped at the Pratt Street Ale House for some food. I wanted to try some local beers as well. Since the car was parked, why not enjoy some local brews? The Pratt Street Ale House is located where else but at 206 W. Pratt Street in Baltimore. I enjoyed the beers and even got a growler to go. I always enjoy local places better than chain restaurants. It had a chill atmosphere, and it was nice to chat with Delia, Sophia, and Ian.

In the evening, we walked around the Inner Harbor of Baltimore. The city had an ice-skating rink set up near the water. I thought more Christmas lights would be set up, but it was still festive. There was a setup with shops and some amusement rides, but they were already taken down after Christmas. The harbor is formed by the Patapsco River, which connects to the Chesapeake Bay. Since the Chesapeake then connects to the Atlantic Ocean, the Inner Harbor is affected by the tides. The water around the shopping area and aquarium had an oily look to it.

The next day the kids wanted to visit the aquarium. What trip to Baltimore is complete without a visit to The National Aquarium? Although tickers are not cheap, it is well worth it. I cannot do justice in describing the setup. Visitors are essentially surrounded by different varies of fish. Since kids were out of school, the aquarium was crowded on the day of our visit. With everything going on in my life, I found staring at the different fish, sharks, and jellyfish to be peaceful. Once I get a place of my own, I want to either set up a nice aquarium or get a cat. That is usually the move of a divorced dad. After spending a few hours looking at the fish, we had to head back to New Jersey.

Some random bits of conversation with my children on our trip to Baltimore:

> "Are we heading south? I thought Maryland was in New England."
> "Geography isn't my strongest subject."
> "What's a cheapskate crab cake? Never mind, it says Chesapeake."
> "Nancy Pelosi was born in Baltimore. I cannot tell if people hate her or like her."
> "Is the Inner Harbor a river or a lake?"
> "Babe Ruth runs funny. He looks top-heavy."

As we left Baltimore, I still couldn't decide if the city is more of a northern or southern state. Technically, its boundaries fall below the Mason-Dixon Line. The people were friendly but not in a Carolina or Georgia way. However, I found the people of Baltimore didn't have the edge that we seem to have in New Jersey. The waitresses at the Waffle House were nice and greeted each customer as they entered the restaurant. The gentleman working the Babe Ruth Museum was friendly but did not seem interested in going out of his way to answer questions. The woman at the front desk at the Hyatt was probably the most outgoing in a southern sort of way. Her last name was Moody, but she was extremely courteous, polite, and seemed proud of Baltimore. She said the jellyfish exhibit was her favorite at the aquarium. I should have asked her if she was from Maryland.

The visit to the Babe Ruth Birthplace and Museum was well worth it. The story of Babe Ruth is legendary and almost unbelievable at times. The fact that he was born in his grandmother's house dropped off at a reform school at age seven, and then somehow becomes one of the greatest baseball players of all time is remarkable. Ruth is the underdog who made it big. He lived the American dream. No other athlete in the 20th Century compares to Babe Ruth. Not Ali or Jordan or even Tom Brady with all his Super Bowl rings. If you ask any fan who is the first person they think of when it comes to baseball, the answer is always Babe Ruth. The visit to Baltimore was a great way to spend time with Delia, Sophia, and Ian while taking in a bit of history.

On the ride back to New Jersey, my children and I shared some jokes. My son tried out his Babe Ruth impression (he is good at mimicking voices). The traffic was horrible on I-95, but it did not matter. What was the rush? I don't know if this was normal traffic or due to the holidays. We enjoyed our brief stay in Baltimore. I would like to go back again to see the Phillies play the Orioles at Camden Yards. Just for the heck of it, on the way home, we stopped at another Waffle House in Havre De Grace, Maryland.

"Can I get a waffle?"

"Yes!"

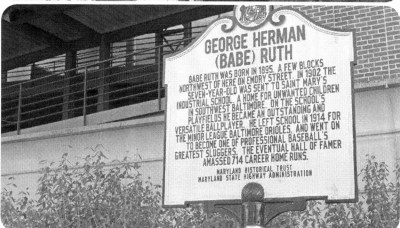

2
COOPERSTOWN

FEBRUARY 8–9, 2020

"Are we still going?"

"Yes, I already booked the hotel room."

"Okay, I'll be ready to go," my son said. We agreed I would pick him up early on Saturday morning. I scheduled our trip on the weekend with nothing else going on. The plan was simple. I would drive north on I-81 until we hit New York. After reaching New York, it was just a few turns, and we would reach Cooperstown by lunchtime.

On February 7, 2020, a weather advisory was given for Upstate New York. The weather forecast called for strong winds, freezing temperature, and a few inches of snow. Events were being canceled, restaurants closed early so their staff could avoid the roads, and it was suggested not to travel except for the case of an emergency. Cooperstown, located in Upstate New York, is more of a village than a town. What better time to head north to visit the National Baseball Hall of Fame and Museum with Ian than on February 8th? We headed out from South Jersey at around 6:45 am on Saturday intending to reach Cooperstown by noon. A little snow couldn't deter our trip!

Baseball did not originate in Cooperstown, New York. The game as we know it was not invented by Abner Doubleday in a cow pasture in 1839. Doubleday was a Civil War general who is often credited with coming up with the rules of the modern-day game. The only problem is that there are no facts to support this claim. Doubleday was in West Point when he was supposedly in Cooperstown sketching out a baseball diamond in the dirt. Why let the truth stand in the way of a good story?

America's Pastime had a problem. The Mills Commission was formed in 1905 to find the origin of baseball. The commission was looking for a story other than the sport evolved from cricket over time. The game of baseball needed to be more American and not of British origin. A man named Abner Graves wrote a letter stating he was present in 1839 at Cooperstown when Doubleday etched a baseball diamond in the dirt. The Mills Commission decided that this version of events was valid and determined Cooperstown was the birthplace of baseball as we know it today. Doubleday never mentioned baseball in any of his memoirs. There is a great book called *Cooperstown Confidential* by Zev Chafets, which explains the murky history of the Hall of Fame.

By the early 1930s, the Village of Cooperstown felt it could capitalize on this story to bring tourists to its town. It is a beautiful area with rolling green hills and a perfect view of Otsego Lake. It is somewhere between New York City and Buffalo, New York. Not exactly a place people would flock to unless they had a reason to go. So, the town decided to build a museum to honor baseball hoping that fans would travel to their quaint village in Upstate New York. Cooperstown's investment paid off. As the 100th anniversary of the birth of baseball approached in 1939, the town had a celebration. People arrived in droves to meet baseball legends such as Babe Ruth and Ty Cobb.

Living in New Jersey, I am a little biased regarding the origins of baseball as we know it today. However, I believe the game originated in Hoboken, New Jersey, on June 19, 1846. In Hoboken, the New York Base Ball Club defeated the Knickerbockers 23–1 at Elysian Fields. Alexander Cartwright umpired the game. On this date in New Jersey, the first organized game was played under rules on par with today's ballgame.

Our connection with the past is sometimes blurry. I think back to my childhood and going to baseball games at Veterans Stadium in Philadelphia. During the early 1980s, the Phillies had such greats as Steve Carlton, Mike Schmidt, Garry Maddox, Pete Rose, and Tug McGraw. Even though The Vet was not a classic ballpark, it created some lasting memories for fans from 1971 to 2003. The only problem with my reflection on the Veterans Stadium is that I hardly went to any games as a child. It wasn't until I started going myself with friends or my own family that I attended Phillies games. Maybe that is why I try and take my three kids to see the Phillies or different minor league ballclubs. I am trying to recreate my past. It doesn't matter much. Just like the creation of baseball in Cooperstown in 1839, sometimes the past or our memories don't have to be perfect when it comes to the actual details.

In 1936, the National Baseball Hall of Fame and Museum was established with the players: Ty Cobb, Walter Johnson, Christy Mathewson, Babe Ruth, and Honus Wagner. I am not sure how Cy Young and his 511 wins as a pitcher was left off the inaugural class. In 1939, the Hall of Fame and Museum officially opened its doors to the public. Although the myth of the beginning of baseball may be in doubt, this is a perfect setting for visiting the game's history. Everything is perfect. Doubleday Field was also established as a ballpark to host various ballgames. The Hall of Fame Game began in 1940 and was played for several decades at Doubleday Field.

Stephen C. Clark founded the Hall of Fame in 1936. His family were prominent citizens in Cooperstown, dating back to the 1800s. Clark was an attorney who made his initial fortune through the partnership of the

Singer Sewing Machine Company. The Clark family purchased several large tracts of land in and around Otsego County. As I write these words, the Clark family still is very much involved with The National Baseball Hall of Fame. Jane Forbes Clark is the chairperson of the board of directors. The Hall of Fame is run as a non-profit organization. Former MLB players are on the board and Joe Morgan, Phil Niekro, Ozzie Smith, Brooks Robinson, and Cal Ripken Jr.

Winter can sometimes be draining on a person. It gets dark early. For work, I get up and warm up my car for a few minutes. The heater never works properly in my Dodge Journey. The winter of 2020 was especially depressing. My wife and I met with the divorce mediator for the first time on January 18, 2020. It was tough. We have three children, own a home, and have been together for more than 20 years. How do you know if you are making the right decision? How does any person know what is right and what is wrong? Sometimes a person can think he or she is making the right move but still have questions.

I planned the trip to Cooperstown just to do something. Sometimes just the planning of a trip can lift a person's spirits. Between the impeachment trial, the 2020 presidential debates, and the Coronavirus, I needed to focus on something positive. Plus, spring training for the Phillies was just a week away. The return of baseball was around the corner (or so I thought at the time). There is nothing better than hearing that pitchers and catchers report to Clearwater, Florida, in less than a week.

Hotel rooms in the middle of winter in upstate New York are relatively inexpensive. We found a Holiday Inn Express for less than $100 just a few miles from Main Street in Cooperstown. Plus, it had an indoor pool and a free breakfast. The Hall of Fame is not expensive to visit. I thought a four-hour car ride with my son would help clear my head. Ian was looking forward to the trip as well. Although the NFL is probably his favorite sport, baseball is a close second. He has played Little League baseball since he was about six years old.

William Cooper founded the Village of Cooperstown. His son James Fennimore would later game fame for writing the book *The Last of the Mohicans*. A visit to the Hall of Fame has always been on my radar for a long time. It has been a place that I should have visited earlier in life. Regrets? I suppose I've had a few. In addition to the Hall of Fame, Cooperstown is also home to the Fenimore Art Museum, The Farmer's Museum, and the Glimmerglass Festival.

The National Baseball Hall of Fame and Museum is a timeless, brick building that has undergone several renovations over the years. The last renovation took place in 2005 at the cost of $20-million and added 10,000 square feet for baseball fans. Renovations also took place in 1950, 1958, 1968, 1980, 1989, and 1994. Inside the building is also the Hall of Fame Library and the A Bartlett Giamatti Research Center. The library has a file on every single player who has appeared in a Major League Baseball Game. More than 15,000 people have played in at least one game since 1875. Everyone from Hank Aaron to Tony Zych has a file. Although our visit was brief, I know I will be back to spend more time in the museum and its library.

To put a monetary value on the contents inside the building is practically impossible. Are the historic gloves, balls, bats, and uniforms worth $100 million? $200 million? Former Yankees pitcher David Wells once bought a cap worn by Babe Ruth for $35,000. In 2012 Wells sold the cap through an auction house for $537,278.40. On a side note, Wells wore the cap in a game against the Cleveland Indians. If just one Yankees cap worn by Ruth is worth half a million dollars, how can one put a figure of the contents inside the Baseball Hall of Fame?

As the sun was just peeking through the morning, we began our journey to the National Baseball Hall of Fame. Ian and I passed through the Pocono Mountains on our way to Cooperstown. We sped by towns with names like Jim Thorpe, Bear Creek, Mountain Top, and Clarks Summit. Ian asked about Pete Rose and if he would ever make it into the Hall of Fame. It was nice to talk some baseball and hear his views on the game. We stopped at a truck stop on the way to New York to load up on Mountain Dew and Doritos. With the snow and the soot, I had to wipe off the windshield as well. I could barely see out of the front windshield!

What struck me about Main Street in Cooperstown is that it could have been from *It's a Wonderful Life* or the television show *Leave it to*

Beaver. I half-expected a young Jerry Mathers to come bouncing down the street while pulling a sled. The town has held on to its early American charm. I didn't see one 7-Eleven or Wawa located in the middle of town. Of course, since it is a baseball town, every store promoted, sold, or advertised something related to America's Pastime. We did not eat yet, so we grabbed lunch at the Doubleday Café located a few doors down from the Hall of Fame. Since this was a mini-vacation, I ordered a local beer. I tried a dark beer from Ommegang Brewery, which is located outside of town. Ian settled for a soda.

The first thing that struck me about Upstate New York is how pleasant the people we met were during the trip. Compared to our visit to Baltimore, New York had a Midwest *niceness* about it. The waitresses, the hotel clerks, the ushers at the Hall of Fame, everyone was so nice. The people took pride in their hometowns. It seems that the farther away from the I-95 corridor, the more pleasant people seem to be. There has been a lot of talk about Major League Baseball eliminating a few dozen minor league teams. That mindset doesn't make sense to me. Baseball is such a big part of many small towns in places like Elmira and Binghamton, New York.

Ian said the people "look like Mississippi but talk like Minnesota." I think I knew what he meant. People think of New York, and they immediately have images of New York City residents. We think Jerry Seinfeld, Spike Lee, Rudy Giuliani, Mr. Met, and Jay-Z. However, when it comes to baseball and New York City, we think of George Steinbrenner, Reggie Jackson, or Darryl Strawberry. New York City is a place I may want to visit, but I would never want to live there. Major cities are too congested for me. Upstate New York is completely different. And it is for the better. I could see myself tending to a small farm and mixing with the locals. I could work the farm and attend baseball games nearby to see the Binghamton Rumble Ponies. A few years back, I visited Binghamton to watch the team play when we were vacationing in the Finger Lakes Region of New York.

At the hotel, I had picked up a copy of The Freeman's Journal. I love to read the local newspaper when on vacation. This local paper has a circulation of about 1,500 and has been around for more than 200 years. William Cooper established it in 1808. Some of the headlines in the February 6th edition included "Daughters, Daddies Dance!", "2020 Carnival Arrives – Bring on the Mac and Cheese", and a short article about a petition started to save the local high school football team. It was refreshing to read the news that didn't include another shooting in Philadelphia or how New Jersey was looking at options to increase taxes again.

Entering the Hall of Fame, any baseball fan immediately feels a connection to baseball's past. It's incredible to think how many legends passed through the front door. Since I am a Phillies fan, I wanted to see the plaques of Mike Schmidt and Richie Ashburn. Plus, I wanted to see the plaque of Effa Manley. She is the first woman inducted into the Hall of Fame and has a connection to New Jersey. Manley ran the Newark Eagles with her husband in the Negro Leagues throughout the 1930s and 1940s.

The museum has expanded several times over the years. Although it is all connected, the building itself has three different main areas. We started on the third floor and worked our way down. The museum also has a theater and a gift shop. The ushers are all helpful. One of the cool things for kids is the scavenger hunt. Ian was given a paper with some clues and searched for the answers throughout the Baseball Hall of Fame. He was really into looking at the exhibits to find the answers to the questions. There is so much history in the Hall of Fame; I could barely wrap my head around it. One of the first things I saw was a statue of Buck O'Neil as I entered the one hallway. O'Neil was a player, coach, and humanitarian. He was such a great ambassador for not only baseball but for life itself.

We also wanted to check out the exhibit for Latin American ballplayers. The game has become a truly international game. I wish I could have seen players such as Roberto Clemente roam the outfield for the Pittsburgh Pirates. Baseball is truly an international game. Clemente was the first Hispanic player to make it into the Hall of Fame. He was inducted in 1973, a year after his tragic death. One of my favorite players growing up was Manny Trillo. He played second base for the Phillies from 1979 to 1982. I liked the quiet, unassuming way he went about his business. He is not in the Hall of Fame, but I always liked his style of play.

Another exhibit that caught my interest was its Shoebox Treasures on baseball cards. The exhibit opened on May 25, 2019, with 700 square feet of space. I grew up during the 1980s when baseball cards were still quite popular. The 1985 Dwight Gooden rookie card was something every kid wanted in his collection. The Hall of Fame exhibit had such rare cards as the 1952 Mickey Mantle and the T206 Honus Wagner. The Wagner card is probably the most famous for it can sell for more than $1 million. One of the fun aspects of the exhibit was making your baseball card from different years.

Our visit to the Hall of Fame coincided with the Houston Astros scandal. How far did the Astros go to win the World Series in 2017? It seems that Houston was using a camera in the outfield to relay the catcher's sign to the hitters. The signal would get relayed to the dugout, where someone would bang on a trash can to tip off the Astros' hitters. This was really cheating to a whole new level. In a way, it tarnished the game. It's funny that this scandal came to light about 100 years after the Chicago White Sox threw the 1919 World Series. In one exhibit, all the MLB teams have a locker on display. Ian and I stopped by the Astros locker. Not that it would happen, but it should have included a trashcan. The whole episode took away some of the innocence of the game of baseball.

The museum was not too crowded since it was February. The few people we did see exploring were primarily New York Yankees fans. The usher said last year it was crazy when Mariano Rivera was inducted into the Hall of Fame. He said people living in town would charge $40 for visitors to park on their lawn. There are worse ways to make some extra money. With 27 World Series Championships, it is no surprise that the Yankees have a ton of memorabilia in Cooperstown.

It was special to see uniforms worn by Babe Ruth and Lou Gehrig. The Hall of Fame and Museum has some unique items as well. One amazing display was a statue of Ruth made entirely out of a block of wood. I took a photo of it, but my camera does not do it justice. Artist

Armand LaMontagne created the sculpture, and the likeness is uncanny. The statue of Ruth in his Yankees pinstripes is of the Babe in his prime.

Ruth was unique in that he was an elite pitcher for the Boston Red Sox before transitioning to the New York Yankees slugger. In 1916 he went 23–12 with a 1.75 ERA for the Red Sox. Ruth followed up in 1917 by going 24–13 with a 2.01 ERA. If he never became "The Babe" hitting home runs but remained a pitcher, would he still have made his way to Cooperstown? Unless he blew out his elbow, it is fair to say Ruth would have easily reached 300 wins if he remained a pitcher.

The only other player besides Babe Ruth, who has more than ten wins as a starting pitcher and hit more than 50 home runs, is Rick Ankiel. I cannot think of any other players who came close. The situation for Ankiel is rather unique in baseball. He made his debut as a pitcher in 1999, and in his first full season in 2000, he earned 11 wins for the Cardinals. In the postseason, though, he developed the "yips" and was unable to throw strikes.

Ankiel eventually gave up on his career as a pitcher. After a few years in the minors, he remade his career as an outfielder. He played several more seasons with the Cardinals, Royals, Braves, Nationals, Astros, and finally the Mets in 2013. He talked of making a comeback in 2019, but he did not play for any games. His book *The Phenomenon: Pressure, The Yips, and the Pitch that Changed My Life* is well worth reading. He wrote about his struggles and the mental anguish he went through after losing his ability to pitch.

Not quite on the level of Babe Ruth or even Rick Ankiel, I was surprised to see a shirt worn by former Phillies player Eric Bruntlett in the Hall of Fame. Bruntlett completed an unassisted triple play against the New York Mets in a game on August 23, 2009. One display that was special as well was a Phillies and Blue Jays uniform worn by Roy Halladay. He pitched a perfect game for the Phillies on May 29, 2010, against the Miami Marlins. Halladay also pitched a post-season no-hitter against the Cincinnati Reds later that year on October 6th. He was such a great player whose life ended tragically while flying his airplane in 2017. Life is fleeting.

The most impressive place within the Hall of Fame is where all the plaques are featured. One could spend all afternoon reading the names and soaking in the history of the game. It almost felt like walking into a church. Since we visited during the dead of winter, it was eerily quiet. A sense of stillness filled the air. All the legends of the game were on display. Ty Cobb, Jimmie Foxx, Joe DiMaggio, Lou Gehrig, Willie Mays, Hank Aaron, Reggie Jackson, Roberto Clemente, Sandy Koufax, and the list goes on.

As we gazed upon the different plaques, I noticed the Hall of Fame almost has two different tiers of players. A baseball fan thinks of players such as Mantle, Clemente, or Mays, and there is no doubt they belong in Cooperstown. And then there are players such as Luis Aparicio, Freddie Lindstrom (who?), and Phil Rizzuto ("holy cow!"). With a .273 lifetime batting average, Rizzuto benefited from being a 7x World Series winner with the Yankees. The recent selection of Harold Baines opened the debate if the bar was being set lower to accept players. Baines was a good player but not a great one.

This leads to another debate about whether a person's character or suspected use of steroids should keep a player out of the Hall of Fame. The next several years will be fun to watch as players such as Barry Bonds, Alex Rodriguez, and Roger Clemens are considered for selection. The two biggest names not in Cooperstown are Pete Rose and Shoeless Joe Jackson. Entire books can be written about Rose and Jackson and whether they deserve to be in. Personally, I am torn on both players. I believe if Rose sincerely apologized for gambling on baseball, he would have a plaque in Cooperstown. It did not help his cause that A. Bartlett Giamatti passed away before Rose could appeal the decision.

"If Pete Rose bet on his own team to win, how can that be a bad thing?" Ian asked me as we made our way to the exit. "The guy with the most hits in baseball is not in the Hall of Fame. It just doesn't make sense."

"Life doesn't always make sense."

Upon leaving the museum, we took a stroll along Main Street. We stopped in the Cooperstown Bat Company. This company has been making wooden bats since 1981. I love shopping in places that say "Made in the USA" on the label. Some of the bats for sale were vintage style which is fascinating to see how the game has evolved over the years. One of the bats was a replica of Black Betsy that Shoeless Joe Jackson used during his playing days. Unfortunately, my son cannot use wooden bats in his Little League. I hate the ping sound of the bats that kids use in today's game. We bought some souvenirs and went our merry way.

After spending the day at the museum and walking around downtown, Ian and I headed back to the hotel. It was nice to just chill in the hotel room. Sometimes, just spending time with family and friends in a low-key way is more enjoyable than running around Disney World or standing in line at a buffet on a cruise ship. It's the simple things. I had a few beers in the room while Ian scrolled through whatever kids scroll through on his phone. Outside, the ground was covered in a blanket of snow.

Around 6 pm or so, we wanted to grab some dinner. Down the road, about a quarter of a mile, was the Council Rock Brewery. From the outside, it did not look like much. However, once inside, we were treated to some great food. Ian is a vegan, but he enjoyed his bean burger. I went with the delicious fish tacos. Due to the snow, the place was closed on Friday. The special of the day was their Friday Fish Fry. They were serving up some of the largest fillets of Haddock I have ever seen. The beers on tap went down smooth. Our server Kyle took a genuine pleasure in describing the different beers they brewed on site. I have nothing against Applebee's, but I will choose a local place serving fresh food and micro-beers over a chain restaurant anytime. It felt like we were eating in a friend's kitchen. The people were so welcoming, and the atmosphere was perfect. One could tell that the locals would visit this place regularly. The hotel clerk even said she goes there about two or three days a week. I took a growler of a local brew to go, and we headed back to the Holiday Inn.

It is incredible to think of all the famous men and women who have visited the National Baseball Hall of Fame and Museum throughout the years. Barack Obama became the first sitting president when he visited in 2014. In his speech, he stated: "So I love baseball; America loves baseball. It continues to be our national pastime. And for any baseball fan out there, you've got to make a trip here." His words echoed true. Despite the iffy weather, Ian and I were glad we made the trip to Cooperstown. Not only did we enjoy the baseball history, but it was nice to spend time together on our little road trip. I hope Ian will look back on this trip and one day tell his children that his dad took him to the Hall of Fame in 2020.

I would like to return to Cooperstown in the summer. It must be crazy with all the people during the weekends with baseball tournaments. One can only imagine the days when a ballplayer is getting inducted as well. However, the town has a lot more to offer than just the National Baseball Hall of Fame and Museum. The area is beautiful, with plenty of restaurants and breweries. Since the weather was so cold during our visit, it was not ideal for exploring the town. The upside to going in February is that we avoided the crowds and could take our time exploring the different exhibits. I would like to go back and see The Farmers Museum and sample some local beers at Brewery Ommegang. Also, it would be fun to have a baseball catch with Ian on Doubleday Field. Maybe we can connect with the ghost of Abner Doubleday. Ask him what he knows about baseball.

Back in the hotel room, we relaxed for a bit and watched the XFL on the television. The hotel was probably only half full. Ian wanted to visit the indoor pool, so we put our bathing suits on and relaxed in the hot tub for a bit. As we walked past the quiet lobby, the clerk at the front desk was aimlessly scrolling through her phone. It felt like we had the entire hotel to ourselves. The warmth of the jacuzzi provided instant relaxation. I hope Ian will look back on our trip with fond memories. We did not say much but just enjoyed the stillness of the moment. For one day, all our problems and stress were put on hold.

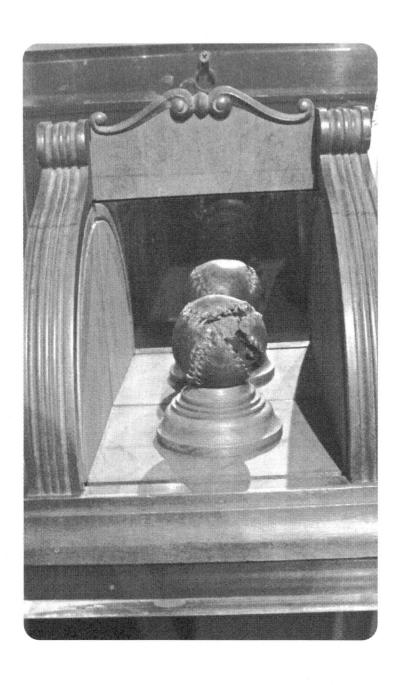

3

LITTLE LEAGUE

EVERY SPRING

The rite of spring. By early March, boys and girls across the United States take to baseball fields to begin practice. The weather is iffy, the fields are still in need of repair, and the coaches try to figure out which kid can catch and hit. Parents make small talk. Some of the dads offer up to help the coach. These are the types of fathers who believe their kid to be the next Mike Trout. The kids show off their new gloves and bats they got for Christmas. Everyone is looking forward to the upcoming season.

"At home, they call me 'Big Al' and I hit dingers."

There is a certain innocence with kids and baseball. Alfred Delia's introduction at the 2018 Little League World Series captured the moment. The solid 12-yeard old from New Jersey confidently announced to the world that he could hit some home runs. The pinnacle for 12-year old boys and girls playing baseball is to reach the Little League World Series (LLWS). Teams from all over the world descend upon Williamsport, Pennsylvania, in August each year to compete.

Watching my son and his team play baseball is one of my favorite activities in the spring and summer months. His teams could never make it to Williamsport. When I was a kid, my teams were never good either. Maybe losing baseball is in our blood. Although Ian has never been on a winning team, watching the kids get better as the season develops is a lot of fun.

Ian is sort of the Ernie "Coach" Pantusso of Little League Baseball. If you remember the television show *Cheers*, Coach had a knack for getting hit by a pitch during his playing days. Ian has the same philosophy at the plate. He once was hit by a pitch in seven out of 9 at-bats. Maybe Ian is more like former Major League player Hughie Jennings who was hit 51 times during the 1896 season. This chapter is not about a specific trip but rather a summary of several trips parents make to their own Little League field. Any mother or father who has a child playing baseball or softball knows the commitment to the sport. Every spring, I look forward to the visits two or three days a week to the ballfield to watch my son play baseball.

Carl Stotz first sparked the idea of baseball for children in 1938. He lived in Williamsport and wanted to create an organized league for pre-teenage boys. Stotz did not have children of his own but often played baseball with his two nephews Jimmy and Major Gehron. In 1938 he experimented with different dimensions for the field with his nephews and some of the neighborhood boys.

By 1939 the first season of Little League Baseball was created with three teams. The kids had their own uniforms and were sponsored by local businesses. The first official game was played on June 6, 1939, with Lundy Lumber defeating Lycoming Dairy. The board of directors was made up of eight members of the community. On the 1939 Lycoming Dairy team was Allen "Sonny" Yearick. He would become the first Little League player to play professional baseball with the Boston Braves organization. Yearick played in their minor league organization for four years. He just recently passed away in January 2020.

In 1947 Hammonton, New Jersey became the first Little League set up outside of Pennsylvania. Hammonton, located in Atlantic County, is known as the "blueberry capital of the world." Hammonton won the Little League World Series in 1949, defeating Pensacola, Florida. The tournament now features teams from all over the world. Monterey, Mexico, was the first team outside the United States to win the championship. The team captured the title in 1957.

Taiwan became the first LLWS juggernaut starting with its first championship in 1969. Their dominance lasted for about 20 years. Taiwan has a total of 17 titles, with their last coming in 1996. From 1971 to 1981, Taiwan racked up a total of nine championships. The Taiwanese players dominated the 1970s more than the Big Red Machine and The Mustache Gang of Oakland in Major League Baseball. Ching-Hui Huang of Taiwan threw a perfect game in 1973. By the 1980s, ESPN started to expand the coverage of the LLWS.

Once ESPN started doing full broadcasts of the rounds leading up to the LLWS championship, I feel some of the innocence was taken from the game. ESPN, EPSN2, and ABC all ended up broadcasting games. The increased visibility creates a lot of pressure for kids playing baseball. Maybe the kids and their families enjoy the experience. It just seems like the added exposure is setting them up for failure. But maybe I am just overthinking it. Games are won. Games are lost. Not everyone can be a winner. Not everything or every moment in baseball or life is perfect. Sometimes it is okay to drop the ball, so to speak.

For the first time in its history, the LLWS was canceled in 2020 due to the COVID-19 pandemic. The decision had a huge impact on Williamsport, which has hosted the LLWS since 1947. Each year more than 300,000 people flock to the city in Lycoming County to watch teams worldwide compete for the championship. In addition to the LLWS cancellation, the MLB Little League Classic was also canceled for 2020. This game features two Major League Baseball teams playing at the BB & T Ballpark at Bowman Field since 2017.

BB & T Ballpark at Bowman Field sits along the banks of Lycoming Creek. The ballpark's construction was completed in 1926, and it is currently the second oldest ballfield in operation in minor league baseball. The first team to take the field was the Williamsport Grays in the New York-Penn League. The team currently occupying the ballpark is the Williamsport Crosscutters. The team was a minor league affiliate of the Phillies. It is now part of the MLB Draft League which showcases collegiate players.

The Crosscutters name is a tip of the cap to Williamsport's past successful lumber industry. At one point in the 19th Century, Williamsport was home to many successful business families who became rich through lumber. One street in Williamsport is known as "Millionaire's Row," as many industrialists had their Victorian-style homes built in this section of the town. Many of these mansions still stand; however, most have been subdivided into apartments or offices. The local high school athletic teams are referred to as the Williamsport Millionaires.

Lycoming County is wedged between the Appalachian Mountains to the west, and a branch of the Susquehanna River cuts through it. The county is located about 125 miles north of Philadelphia. The county is home to Lycoming College, which was established in 1812. One borough within Lycoming County has the unusual name of Jersey Shore. When people think of the *Jersey Shore*, they usually think of Long Beach Island, Wildwood, or Cape May. The Jersey Shore in Pennsylvania is nowhere near the Atlantic Ocean. The town received its name after two early settlers of the area who resettled from New Jersey. Its most famous resident was Hunter S. Thompson, who lived there briefly after leaving the Air

Force. Thompson took a writing job with the Jersey Shore Herald. He found the town rather boring and soon moved on to New York City and eventually Woody Creek, Colorado. Thompson did not last long enough to attend a Little League World Series game. I am not sure he had much interest in baseball anyway.

Quite a few Major League Baseball players traveled through Williamsport on their way to the big leagues. Todd Frazier had great success with the Toms River, New Jersey team in the 1998 LLWS. His team was nicknamed the "Beasts of the East" and defeated the Japanese team 12–9. He not only started the game with a leadoff home run, but Frazier closed out the game as the winning pitcher. Frazier played baseball for Rutgers University before being drafted by the Cincinnati Reds. In addition to the Reds, he has played for the Chicago White Sox, New York Mets, and New York Yankees. He is a 2x All-Star and signed with the Texas Rangers for the 2020 season.

Besides Frazier, some of the other MLB players who appeared in the LLWS include Cody Bellinger (2007), Michael Conforto (2004), Scott Kingery (2006), Gary Sheffield (1980), and Jason Varitek (1984). In a strange twist of fate, Conforto, Frazier, and Kingery would later meet in Williamsport to play baseball. The Mets defeated the Phillies in 2018 at the Little League Classic. The game was played at BB & T Ballpark at Historic Bowman Field.

Varitek has the distinction of playing in the Little League World Series, the College World Series, and the World Series. His Little League team from Altamonte Springs, Florida, lost in the championship game to South Korea. Varitek attended Georgia Tech, where he was a key member of the team that reached the College World Series in 1994. Unfortunately, the Yellow Jackets ended up losing the University of Oklahoma. The pinnacle of his career was with the Boston Red Sox. He was the clubhouse leader and won the World Series Championship twice in 2004 and 2007. Varitek was later elected to the Boston Red Sox Hall of Fame.

Other athletes besides baseball players have made their way through Williamsport. Former NHL player Chris Drury starred in the 1989 Little League World Series. Drury is the only athlete to win an LLWS championship and the Stanley Cup (with the Colorado Avalanche in 2001). Several other NHL players made their way through town as well, including Ray Ferraro (1976), former Montreal Canadien Pierre Turgeon (1982), and Stephane Matteau (1982). Former NFL quarterback Brian Sipe played for the El Cajon, California team in the 1961 LLWS. Journeyman NFL quarterback Matt Cassel played in the Williamsport classic in 1994. Cassel has been a quarterback for several NFL teams, the most recent being the Detroit Lions in 2018. He was drafted by the Oakland Athletics in the 2004 MLB draft but chose football instead. Even NASCAR driver Austin Dillon made a pit stop in Williamsport in 2002 with his Little League team from North Carolina. NASCAR legend Richard Petty cannot make the same claim.

One of the biggest stars in LLWS history was not just a great player but also a trailblazer. Mo'ne Davis became the first girl to record a win by defeating the Nashville team 4–0 in 2014. Davis played for the Taney Dragons from the Philadelphia area. Her fastball clocked in at 70 mph, and she had great accuracy with her pitches. She became something of a celebrity and appeared on the front cover of Sports Illustrated. Davis even threw the ceremonial first pitch before Game 4 of the 2014 World Series. Many sports celebrities praised her for creating her own path in the game of baseball. Davis also excelled on the basketball court as well. Throughout the media blitz, she kept her poise and head about her. After high school, she started playing softball for Hampton University in Virginia.

Davis was not the first girl to play Little League. Maria Pepe of New Jersey played for her local team in 1972. After the Little League organization sought to revoke the team's status, a lawsuit was filed on her behalf. Unfortunately, Pepe turned in her uniform; otherwise, the team would not be able to play. The New Jersey Superior ruled in her favor as the case gained national attention. The decision ushered in an era where thousands of girls signed up to play baseball. Pepe is remembered as a trailblazer for equality in sports. She helped pave the way for players like Mo'Ne Davis, Victoria Roche, and Maddie Freking.

The other player that most people remember from Little League is Danny Almonte. In the 2001 Little League World Series tournament,

Almonte allowed only a handful of hits, struck out 62 batters, and was so dominant that other teams questioned his actual age. He also tossed a perfect game. It was too good to be true. It turns out, it was too good to be true. His Dominican birth certificate was a fake. Almonte was 14-years old, which is two years older than the permitted age. As a result, his statistics were erased from the record books, and his team, Rolando Paulino All-Stars of New York, had to forfeit their games.

In a way, it is sad that Almonte took such heat for the controversy. He was still just a 14-year-old kid who only spoke Spanish. Was he merely a pawn in the game of Little League Baseball? It seems that the adults he trusted took advantage of him. He would later become an excellent high school pitcher. At 19 years of age and a senior in high school, he was married to a 30-year-old woman. Despite being a star pitcher in high school, he was passed on being drafted by any MLB team. Almonte pitched six games for an independent team in the Frontier League in 2007. His professional pitching career stats were 0–1 with a 5.28 ERA. ESPN featured him in a "30 for 30" feature show titled "Kid Danny."

My own Little League baseball career came to an end at 12 years old. Even as a 14-year-old, I could not have competed with the 12-year-old kids. The scouting report on me was: "slow, weak arm, limited range, makes contact but struggles to hit it out of the infield, weak fielder, but pleasant demeanor on the bench." I played for a small league called Catalina Hills Little League. The two fields and snack bar were tucked away in a residential neighborhood. My team never played in any tournaments outside New Jersey. I do not even remember any tournaments even outside our county. This was the early 1980s when leagues did not hand out participation trophies. My team could have used a few players such as Mo'Ne Davis or Alfred Delia to help us earn a few extra wins.

Outside of the Little League World Series, Mike Mussina is probably the most famous baseball player from the Williamsport area. During his career, Mussina played for the Orioles and then famously (or infamously if you are from Baltimore) signed with the New York Yankees. Mussina graduated from Montoursville Area High School before going on to play baseball for Stanford University.

Nicknamed "Moose," Mussina was drafted by the Orioles and made his debut for the team in 1991. He spent the first ten years of his career in Baltimore. He routinely threw more than 200 innings a season. Mussina left via free agency for the Yankees, where he finished his career. Despite winning 20 games in 2008, he retired after the season. His final year was the only season he was a 20-game winner. Mussina finished with a 270–153 record and an ERA of 3.68 over 18 seasons. He was a durable workhorse of a pitcher who did not crave the limelight. Mussina was the first pitcher since Sandy Koufax to retire after a 20-win season. If Mussina hung around for another two seasons, could he have reached 300 wins?

Quiet and unassuming, in 2019, the former Montoursville resident and Hall of Fame pitcher returned to Williamsport to attend at Bowman Field before a Crosscutters game. He signed autographs and met with the fans. Mussina was elected to the Baseball Hall of Fame in the same year. Although not an elite pitcher like Pedro Martinez or Roger Clemens, Mussina was consistent over his great career, a 5x All-Star, and 7x Gold Glove winner. This small-town hero deserved his plaque in Cooperstown.

Little League is not the oldest youth baseball format in the United States. The idea for American Legion Baseball was formed in 1925 at a convention in South Dakota. In 1926, American Legion posts in 15 different states established baseball tournaments for teenage boys. Part of the goal was to teach "citizenship through sportsmanship." Their first championship series was held in Philadelphia, with a team from Yonkers, New York, taking the title. A national tournament was not held in 1927; however, one has taken place every year since 1928. The American Legion provides players between the ages of 13–19 years of age to play highly competitive baseball during summer.

Near my hometown in South Jersey is the Brooklawn American Legion team. Under the leadership of Dennis Barth, the Brooklawn team has won several National Championships. Barth helped create a powerhouse of a team starting in 1991–2015. As a result, this tiny borough of fewer than 2,000 residents near the Delaware River has become a baseball powerhouse.

American Legion baseball has seen several of its players move on to play Major League Baseball. Some of the biggest names in baseball have suited up for an American Legion team. These names include Yogi Berra, Ted Williams, Frank Robinson, Dusty Baker, Albert Pujols, and Chipper Jones. One of the biggest fans of American Legion baseball was Bob Feller. He became a teenage pitching phenomenon who went on to have a Hall of Fame career with the Cleveland Indians. He missed several of his prime years due to military service during World War II. Despite missing three seasons, he finished his career with 266 wins and a 3.25 ERA.

In the last ten years or so, American Legion Baseball has lost some of its influence. By the 1940s, American Legions posts throughout the United States sponsored nearly 7,000 teams. As of this writing, nearly half of those teams no longer exist. Unfortunately, travel baseball programs and showcase teams have become the norm for young, talented ballplayers. Parents now invest thousands of dollars so their kids can play travel baseball. Kids now make trips to Orlando, Florida, to play in weeklong tournaments. I was looking to sign Ian up for a local travel team that guaranteed several tournaments in other states. Unfortunately, the cost was $1,700, which did not include travel, lodging, and other expenses. I just could not afford the cost and ended up signing him up for a local youth club. In addition to American Legion losing kids to the travel teams, other sports such as lacrosse and spring soccer have increased in popularity. American Legion Baseball still rolls along with each summer, though despite the competition.

Within the last ten years, several different articles have been written about the decline of baseball with the younger generation. Also, the average age of the MLB fanbase is much older compared to the NBA and the NFL. Kids who now grow up playing video games such as *Madden NFL* want fast-paced games. The television ratings for the World Series have been declining since 1995. The popular refrain about baseball is "it's too slow" and "the games take too long." Baseball, in a way, has become like the NHL. It is a regional sport. Fans will watch their local baseball or hockey team; however, they will not tune in to watch two teams outside their hometown region. All this may be true; however, baseball still has a prominent place in American culture.

One thing which a person rarely sees these days is a pick-up game of baseball. In the iconic move *The Sandlot*, the kids routinely meet up on their neighborhood ballfield to play some baseball. A pick-up game of baseball at the local park never happens these days. One hardly ever sees kids practicing baseball on their own without an adult nearby. Kids will shoot hoops or play street hockey, but for baseball, it is different. In today's times, Squints, Ham, Smalls, and Yeah-Yeah would not be found hitting flying balls at the neighborhood field. For baseball, it seems that more young boys and girls are pushed into organized play.

It should be noted that kids still play baseball. Many of my son's friends still play baseball in different leagues. These kids fall in the 11–13year old age range. Although dek hockey and lacrosse are quite popular in New Jersey, baseball still has a place in youth sports. According to reports, 25 million boys and girls played either baseball or softball as recently as 2018. Also, as parents worry more about concussions, it will be interesting to see if kids start to move away from football and gravitate back towards baseball.

Major League Baseball has also taken an interest in reviving the game with its Reviving Baseball in Inner Cities (RBI) Program. The program was established in 1991 to get more young people from the inner cities to start playing baseball and softball. Many of the major league teams have implemented their version of the program. The Philadelphia Phillies created the Phillies Jr. RBI Program to get children in Philadelphia, New Jersey, and Delaware to start playing baseball.

In 2015 MLB initiated its "Play Ball" marketing plan to increase the participation of both softball and baseball throughout the United States. This push did not just include the inner-cites but the suburbs and rural areas as well. The goal was not just to have kids play baseball but to increase their physical activity as well. This initiative included fun events such as a Jr. Home Derby and Pitch, Hit & Run. Since its inception, the game has seen an increase in kids wanting to play baseball.

The year 2020 caused youth sports to hit the pause button. I know my son's Little League team shut down practice in mid-March. A month later, the decision was made to cancel the spring season. As mentioned earlier, the Little League World Series was canceled for the first time since its inception. Youth baseball, however, is far from dead. Kids will soon return to the game. Just as kids have played baseball for the last 150 years, the sport will continue to have a place in our society.

While working on this book, I went back to my old Little League field. It is at the end of Pasadena Drive in Magnolia, New Jersey. The two fields were still there. The league I played for is no longer around, but a new organization now uses these fields today. One is a smaller field for younger kids. The other is for the bigger kids, probably those players in the 12–14-year-old age range. Even though the park is less than a mile from my home, it was probably more than 30 or so years since I visited these fields. A lot of fun memories crept back into my mind. The snack bar was still standing. Baseball provides such a link to one's past. I thought back to my dad coaching a few of my teams. I thought back to some of my old teammates. I did not keep in touch with any of them. They now have children of their own. A few of them probably even have grandchildren playing t-ball. I wondered if any of them ever come back to relive old memories like myself. Hopefully, they look back on their baseball days with fondness, too.

There is a lot more to baseball than wins and losses. And I do not get caught up in a player's statistics. In the original movie *The Bad News Bears*, the two teams gathered at the end of the championship game. The Yankees received their 4-foot-tall championship trophy. The Bears looked discouraged at first as they watched their opponents celebrate. However, all was not lost. As little Lupus said before tossing their tiny second-place trophy into the dirt: "And another thing, just wait 'till next year!"

There is always next year.

4

JUDY JOHNSON

MAY 17, 2020

History can be found in your own backyard. Or, in this case, Delaware.

Some of the great names in baseball include Ty, Honus, Mickey, Jackie, Willie, Roberto, Hank, Nolan, Reggie, Cal, Chipper, and Judy. All these players are in the Hall of Fame. If the name Judy does not exactly ring a bell, he was one of the greatest third basemen in history. Judy Johnson played in the Negro Leagues from 1921 to 1937. Although he was born in Snow Hill, Maryland, his family moved to Delaware when he was a young child. Johnson is the first person from Delaware elected to the Baseball Hall of Fame. He resided for many years in Marshallton, a small, blue-collar community located in New Castle County, Delaware. The home he shared with his wife Anita is just a few miles outside Wilmington and listed in the National Register of Historic Places.

Before the world turned on its head, 2020 was supposed to be a special year for commemorating Negro League Baseball. On February 13, 1920, Rube Foster brought together a few other owners of Black baseball teams in Kansas City, Missouri. He intended to organize the teams and provide some structure. Foster's leadership provided the birth of the Negro National League. Foster was a good player, but he was an even better executive. He was elected to the Baseball Hall of Fame in 1981. In 2020 Major League Baseball was scheduled to have various events to celebrate the 100th Anniversary of Negro League Baseball. Unfortunately, with COVID-19, Major League Baseball was essentially shut down for the fans to visit the ballparks. Even the Negro League Baseball Museum had to shut down on March 14, 2020, due to the coronavirus.

Most kids are not interested in local history. It is too boring. Young people would rather focus on their iPhones, Tik Tok, or the latest outfit of Kendall Jenner. I was the same way as a child. When PAC-MAN came out in the early 1980s, I constantly asked my mom for quarters if we walked by a game. In Wildwood, New Jersey, there is an arcade with Ms. PAC-MAN. I still find myself feeding a few quarters into the machine if I happen to walk by. I cannot help it. With that being said, I try and instill in Delia, Sophia, and Ian a sense of history.

History was my favorite subject in high school. I attended West Chester University and earned a degree in history. The common thread that connects the past to the present is something I have learned to appreciate in the last 20 years. The history of Negro League baseball has always interested me. Books such as *Curveball: The Remarkable Story of Toni Stone* and *The Negro Leagues of New Jersey* opened my eyes to what these players went through to play baseball. Segregated baseball is not that far in the past. Frank Robinson became the first black person to be hired as a manager in Major League Baseball. And that did not happen until 1975, when the Cleveland Indians hired him. One does not have to look far to see that most managers hired even today are white in both the National and American League. The same could be said for the lack of Latino managers and coaches as well. Heading into the 2020 season, only Dave Roberts with the Los Angeles Dodgers and Dusty Baker with the Houston Astros are managing Major League Baseball.

A few years ago, I briefly met former Negro League player Robert Scott at a baseball card and memorabilia event at the Wildwood Convention Center. In the middle of tables and displays of various baseball cards, posters, jerseys, signed bats, and balls, Scott sold some photos of himself from his playing days with the New York Black Yankees. He grew up near Macon, Georgia, but he signed with the Black Yankees as a teenager in 1946. Scott played for several seasons in the Negro Leagues. After leaving baseball, he settled in New Jersey and worked as a brick layer for more than 30 years. I purchased a baseball card from Scott, which he happily signed for me. This moment led me to think that a person never knows where history may turn up. I have a hard time wrapping my head around Major League Baseball being segregated until Jackie Robinson made his debut with the Brooklyn Dodgers in 1947. Scott talked proudly of playing in Yankee Stadium in front of large crowds. The Yankees, like a lot of ballclubs, leased out their stadium to Negro League teams to bring in extra revenue.

The following year Robert Scott signed a baseball card for me, Greg "The Hammer" Valentine was at the Wildwood Convention Center. I remember watching him wrestle for the WWF on television. During the mid-1980s, Valentine was the Intercontinental Heavyweight Champion. As a kid watching professional wresting on Saturday mornings, the wrestlers all seemed larger than life. Valentine was a lot smaller in person. It was kind of sad seeing him sitting at a table selling autographed photos of himself.

With travel restrictions lifted throughout most of the country, I decided on a road trip to Wilmington, Delaware, on May 17, 2020. I wanted to learn more about a Hall of Fame third baseman from the 1920s. The kids needed to get out of the house as well. With their physical schools shut down, they spend about 20 hours a day in their rooms. My younger daughter Sophia immediately bailed on the trip. Delia and

Ian reluctantly agreed to go. I had to make a promise that we would visit a Waffle House. Spending $20 on gas and $10 on tolls seemed like a lot for a waffle, but it is the price we pay to spend time with our children. As the pandemic restrictions were eased, most Americans seemed to flock to the beaches and parks. I did not feel comfortable rubbing elbows with the public quite yet. Delaware would fit the bill for a social distancing Sunday afternoon.

Delaware is kind of a funny state. It is known as "The First State" since it was the first to ratify the U.S. Constitution. After Rhode Island, it is the smallest state in the country. Three counties make up Delaware: New Castle, Kent, and Sussex. It is a good place to shop since there is no sales tax. People in Delaware believe it should be two states: North Delaware and Lower Delaware. The Chesapeake Delaware Canal is the dividing line. The northern part of the state is made up of Wilmington and more urban areas. The lower part of the state is more rural and easy-going. Bob Marley once lived in Delaware. His son Stephen was born in Wilmington in 1972. However, this chapter is not about the king of reggae music but rather Judy Johnson.

With only 70,000 people, Wilmington is not necessarily a large city. Its population has been in a steady decline since 1950. Wilmington's reputation took a major hit with the riots of 1968. After Martin Luther King, Jr. was assassinated, civil unrest took place in the city. The governor called in the National Guard, which ended up occupying Wilmington for several months. In recent years, several major banking companies have set up large offices within the city limits. DuPont is also a major player not only in Wilmington but throughout Delaware.

Playing in the Negro Leagues, Johnson was often considered one of the greatest third basemen in baseball history. A statue of Johnson stands in front of Frawley Stadium in Wilmington, Delaware. This ballpark is home to the Wilmington Blue Rocks of the Carolina League. The Blue Rocks are a minor league affiliate of the Kansas City Royals. I have been to a few Blue Rocks games over the years; however, I never knew much about Johnson. I am more familiar with some of the bigger names of the Negro Leagues, such as Josh Gibson, Satchel Paige, Cool Papa Bell, and Biz Mackey. I also knew of Pop Lloyd, who lived in Atlantic City for several years. After retiring from baseball, Lloyd assisted with youth baseball leagues in Atlantic City and has a youth ballfield named after him in town.

The Greater-Philadelphia area has a deep history with Negro League Baseball. The Philadelphia Stars were the preeminent team in the area and featured several top-level players during its prime years. The Stars played primarily in the Negro National League and won the Championship over the Chicago American Giants in 1934. Their home field was located at 44th and Parkside, where a large mural is now located highlighting the Stars. I enjoy reading about Philadelphia history and exploring different sites.

Delia, Ian, and I left New Jersey around 11 A.M. and headed south on I-95. Ian already started complaining because he changed his mind and wanted to go home to play video games. The COVID-19 shutdown probably disrupted his life the most. He cannot play with his friends. His birthday party was canceled, his Little League season over after only a few practices, and everything else was turned upside down. Our conversation in the car was the typical talk we normally have on road trips:

"Is there a nice section of Wilmington?"
"Can you turn the radio down? Country music sucks."
"What's the drinking age in Delaware?"
"When is Joe Biden going to pick Kamala Harris?"
"If he is elected, do you think Biden will finish his term?"
"Since Delaware has such low taxes, why don't more people
    move here?"
"Will we have to eat our Waffle House in the parking lot?"
"Can we go home now?"

We pulled up to Frawley Stadium and its empty parking lot. Normally, the Blue Rocks season would be in full swing. It was a bit sad to see the ballpark, not in use. Our family attended a game a few years ago to see "Muggles and Magicians Night" at the park (my guess is the team could not use the words "Harry Potter" due to trademark infringement). My son had Butterbeer. I had Budweiser. The current situation for minor league teams is filled with uncertainty. Most minor league teams only make money if fans are in the seats. They don't have the lucrative television contract of Major League Baseball or make a ton of money from merchandise.

Frawley Stadium is your typical minor league park and located a stone's throw from I-95. My first game to see the Blue Rocks was April 22, 2000 (Section B, Row 1, Seat 13—I saved the ticket stub). The stadium was mostly empty. I cannot remember anything about the game except that Steve Balboni was one of the coaches. Balboni played for the Kansas City Royals for a few years. The only thing I recall about him was that he could hit home runs and had a great mustache. The ballpark is located on Shipyard Drive and surrounded by restaurants, apartments, and a few hotels. The Delaware Children's Museum and The Delaware Contemporary (an art space) are within walking distance.

Frawley Stadium is named after Daniel S. Frawley, who was the mayor of Wilmington. He was instrumental in minor league baseball returning to Delaware. The ballpark can seat 6,400 fans. The Blue Rocks played their first game in Wilmington in 1993. Except for two seasons with the Boston Red Sox, the team has been an affiliate of the Kansas City Royals. Some of the team's alumni include Johnny Damon, Eric Hosmer, Mike Moustakas, and Mike Sweeney. One of my all-time favorite bench players, Sal Fasano, played in Wilmington during the 1994 and 1995 seasons. Fasano played for the Phillies in 2006 and connected with the fans in his lone season. Like Balboni, Fasano had a tremendous mustache. Since arriving in Delaware, the Blue Rocks won the title in 1994, 1996, 1998, 1999, and 2019. Their 20-year drought ended in 2019 when the Blue Rocks defeated the Fayetteville Woodpeckers in five games.

The Judy Johnson statue was unveiled in 1995. Hunched over and with his hands on his knees, Johnson appears to be ready to field a baseball hit his way. The bronze statue was the creation of artist Phil Sumpter. Located at the main entrance to Frawley Stadium, fans cannot miss Judy

Johnson as they enter the ballpark. In addition to the statue, the actual field is referred to as Judy Johnson Field.

After I took a few photos of the statue of Judy Johnson, we headed out to find his former home in Marshallton. Johnson and his wife Anita were married for 62 years and purchased the home in 1934. At the time, he was playing for the Hilldale Club in Darby, Pennsylvania. Marshallton is a suburb of Wilmington named after John Marshall, a mill owner in the 1800s. William Julius Johnson was born in Snow Hill, Maryland. His family moved to Delaware when he was just a child. Johnson received the nickname "Judy" due to his resemblance to another Negro League player named Judy Gans. Although Johnson's father pushed him to be a boxer, the son gravitated more to the sandlots of Wilmington to play baseball with neighborhood kids. The younger Johnson did not take a liking to boxing despite his father being an excellent boxer himself.

Johnson began playing professionally for the Hilldale Club (some-times referred to as the Daisies) in 1921. This baseball team was based in Darby, Pennsylvania, which is about five miles from Philadelphia. He remained with Hilldale from 1921 to 1929 and then returned to play from 1931 to 1932. The Greater-Philadelphia area had enough Black baseball teams that Hilldale did not have to go far to find an opponent. In a way, Johnson was lucky compared to other Negro League players. Since he spent the bulk of his career with the Hilldale Club, he did not have to travel as much as other ball clubs. Buck O'Neil tells stories about traveling by bus all around the country. Teams like the American Giants and Indianapolis Clowns made a living barnstorming around the United States to play baseball.

At 5'11" and weighing 155 pounds, Johnson had a rather slight build for baseball. Compared to players today who are often over 6' and weigh 200 pounds, Johnson would be considered diminutive in the modern game. His frame would be comparable to former pitcher Tim Lincecum, listed as 5'11" and 170 pounds. The Hilldale Club won the champion-ship in 1925 over the Kansas City Monarchs. Hilldale was a powerhouse with Biz Mackey behind the plate and Johnson at third. The Monarchs (and the Homestead Grays) are often considered the elite team of Negro

League Baseball. Despite his size, Johnson was voted the Negro Leagues MVP in 1929 by two prominent Black newspapers- the *Chicago Defender* and the *Pittsburgh Courier.*

At the end of his career, Johnson played for the Pittsburgh Crawfords. The 1935 Crawfords team featured several future Hall of Fame players, including Cool Papa Bell and Josh Gibson. After retiring as a player in 1937, Johnson worked for several MLB teams, including the Philadelphia Athletics, Atlanta Braves, Milwaukee Brewers, Phillies, and the Los Angeles Dodgers. He is often credited with getting the Phillies to sign Dick Allen. Johnson was elected to the Baseball Hall of Fame in 1975.

Johnson's former home was located on the corner of a typical, suburban neighborhood. It was not hard to find; however, I did make a few wrong turns before asking my daughter to check her iPhone for the exact location. Across the street from the home was a church. He lived in this home from 1934 up until he died in 1989. The historical marker sits on the corner of the property. I felt kind of funny taking a photo since the place is a normal residential property occupied by a family (and I do not want to give out the exact address. A quick Google search, though, and anyone can figure it out). So I hopped out of my car and took a few photos of the sign while respecting the privacy of the residence.

Trying to explain segregated baseball to my kids is difficult. My son started getting into baseball and the Phillies just as Ryan Howard was finishing his career. Ian's favorite player was Howard due to the home runs he hit at Citizens Bank Park. I try to tell Ian that if Howard played in the 1930s, Major League Baseball would not have been an option.

"Why not?"

"Black players were not permitted to play."

"How come if they were good enough?"

"Good question. I don't know the answer," I replied.

Judy Johnson, Josh Gibson, Cool Papa Bell, and Buck Leonard were never offered the chance to play Major League Baseball. What would Satchel Paige have done if he started pitching for the Cleveland Indians 20 years earlier? If given a chance, would people say "Judy Johnson is the greatest third baseman of all time" rather than arguing about Mike Schmidt, George Brett, or Brooks Robinson?

Once Jackie Robinson broke the color barrier, it is fascinating to see the National League MVP players from the Negro Leagues. Robinson won the award in 1949. Roy Campanella won in 1951, 1953, and 1955. Willie Mays won in 1954. Don Newcombe won in 1956 as a pitcher. Hank Aaron won in 1957. Ernie Banks won back-to-back titles in 1958 and 1959. Before the color barrier was broken in 1947, Major League Baseball did not have all the best players on the field. The American League was slower to bring in Black baseball players. The Cleveland Indians were the first AL team to sign a Black payer when they signed Larry Doby in 1947. Doby would win the World Series with the Indians in 1948. He was as 7x All-Star and elected to the Baseball Hall of Fame in 1998.

The best thing for Major League Baseball was breaking down the color barrier. After Kenesaw Mountain Landis died in 1944, it was just a matter of time for this unspoken rule to dissipate. Once the top players such as Robinson and Mays signed MLB contracts, this was essentially the end of the Negro Leagues. Even the great organizations such as the Monarchs saw their attendance take a hit. The Indianapolis Clowns were the last Negro League team that continued to play. The Clowns continued to play more as a barnstorming team up until the 1980s. They were also the first team to have a woman play for them when they signed Toni Stone in 1953. Hank Aaron even briefly played for the Clowns in 1952. The Milwaukee Braves ended up purchasing his contract from Indianapolis. Returning to Judy Johnson, he was retired from baseball by the time Black players were permitted to play in the MLB.

In addition to the Baseball Hall of Fame, Johnson was in the inaugural class of the Delaware Sports Hall of Fame in 1976. The Delaware Sports Museum and Hall of Fame is connected to Frawley Stadium and open before Blue Rocks games. Some of the other athletes in the Delaware Hall of Fame include former Phillies manager Dallas Green, Randy White, who played for the Dallas Cowboys, and Montell Owens, who played in the NFL for nine seasons.

On the way home, although in the opposite direction, we stopped at a Waffle House in Maryland. Everything was different since the last time we visited a Waffle House. We could only order take-out and were not permitted to sit inside the restaurant. Each state had its own set of rules when it came to rules regarding the pandemic. I had to put on my face covering, go in, place our order, and then wait outside. I don't mind wearing the face mask. I don't see it as a political issue.

For this trip, I searched out the closest restaurant on their website. One new thing I learned is the Waffle House has its own record label called Waffle Records. The restaurant chain has been recording music for its jukeboxes since 1982. Some of their "hits" include "Waffle House Man" and "Exit 239," which is a nod to a Waffle House in Georgia. One of the Waffle Records producers, Jerry Buckner, also partnered on a few other classic songs such as "Pac-Man Fever" and the theme song for *WKRP in Cincinnati*. Even a few mainstream musicians profess a love for Waffle House. Hootie & the Blowfish named their 2010 album *Scattered, Smothered, and Covered* as a tip of the cap to the popular waffle chain. So the next time I visit the Waffle House and can sit in a booth, I am going to check out the jukebox.

Delia, Ian, and I ate our Waffle House food in the parking lot. The food was good, but it just wasn't the same. The restaurant was next to a gas station. Not exactly great ambiance. We watched trucks and cars pull in to fill up on gas. In New Jersey, we are used to a gas attendant coming out to the car to fill up the gas tank. I believe the Garden State is the only one where people cannot pump their own gas. Part of the fun in eating inside the Waffle House is watching the waitresses and cooks manage 20 different orders. They are like magicians. I do not know how they juggle all the different orders, serve the food so quickly, manage the register and all with a smile.

Ian took a sip of his soda.

"Is this Dr. Pepper?"

"No, it's Mr. Pibb. Waffle House doesn't serve Dr. Pepper."

"Okay, it's all good."

And with that, we slid into the car and headed for home.

WILLIAM JULIUS "JUDY" JOHNSON
October 26, 1899 – June 15, 1989

A resident of Delaware for nearly seventy-five years, Judy Johnson was considered the finest third baseman of his day in the Negro Leagues. After attending Howard High School, he played with the Hilldale Club, Homestead Grays and Pittsburgh Crawfords between 1923 and 1936. A consistent .300 hitter, Judy hit .416 in 1929. Judy was the captain of the 1935 champion Crawfords team which also included Satchel Paige, Cool Papa Bell, Josh Gibson and Oscar Charleston. Following his playing career, Judy remained involved in the game he loved as a coach, scout and mentor. Judy Johnson was enshrined in the Baseball Hall of Fame in 1975.

"The memory of these fellows I will never forget. They were quite a team. We had a lot of fun. There were some sad days, too. But there was always sun shining someplace. So that was what we looked forward to, the big days, the best days."
Judy Johnson, on the 1935 Crawfords

5

FATHER'S DAY

JUNE 21, 2020

Somewhere along the way, something went askew.

As the Billionaire owners argued with the millionaire players, the 2020 Major League Baseball season was put on hold. No one in the negotiations seemed to notice the 40 million Americans who lost their jobs, the people protesting in the streets, or the more than 100,000 who lost their lives to the coronavirus. After the 1994 strike, baseball fans turned away from the game. The sport now trails the NFL and NBA in popularity. Is the current baseball commissioner the worst of the four major sports? One could argue that he did not seem to do enough to bring the two sides together.

Baseball will not completely disappear. For many towns and small-market cities, minor league baseball is an integral part of the community. The Reading Fightin Phils are no exception. Reading is a medium-sized city of 88,000 people in southern Pennsylvania. It is the midway point between Harrisburg (the state capital) and Philadelphia. The Fightin Phils have been a minor league affiliate of the Phillies since 1967.

The Fightin Phils play at FirstEnergy Stadium, which is currently the oldest ballpark in the Eastern League. Built in 1951, FirstEngergy Stadium was originally named Reading Municipal Memorial Stadium. The Cleveland Indians farm team was the first professional tenant starting in 1952. For the first few decades of its existence, little was done regarding updates to the ballpark. However, in 1988, numerous upgrades were done to the ballpark, including adding a picnic area, a food court, building a new grandstand, and adding a $675,000 video scoreboard. The name was also changed due to corporate sponsorship. Most organizations in baseball (both major and minor league teams) have cashed in on changing the name of the ballpark for advertising rights. FirstEnergy Stadium can seat accommodate 9,000 fans for a ballgame. One upgrade that most baseball purists do not appreciate is adding a 1,000 square feet pool behind the right-field fence. Fans can enjoy the game while relaxing in the heated pool. Baseball has been doing more of these types of activities in recent years to appeal to families with young children.

With baseball on hold due to COVID-19 and depending on fans in the seats for income, many minor league teams became creative in generating revenue. The Rocky Mountain Vibes in Colorado Springs, Colorado, started offering curbside takeout to fans and offered a drive-in showing of *Back to the Future* for $20 per vehicle. The Somerset Patriots, a New Jersey independent team, showed *The Sandlot* in its parking lot. This proved successful as the event sold out. The Sussex County Miners, another independent team in New Jersey, hosted events such as a petting zoo and a fireworks night. One event special for the community was the

San Jose Giants hosting drive-through graduation for the Cristo Rey San José Jesuit High School class of 2020. Students drove onto the field to accept their diplomas at home plate on June 6, 2020. The team's mascot was there to offer congratulations!

The Clinton LumberKings held an event showcasing the Axe Women Loggers of Maine at their home ballpark in Clinton, Iowa. The Lumberjill Show featured women professional loggers who chop, saw, use chainsaws, and throw axes. The cost was only $5 for admission. I never knew of professional women loggers touring the country, but I would pay to see it. The Lumberkings were the team featured in a great book called *Class A: Baseball in the Middle of Everywhere* by Lucas Mann. The author spent a season with the team and delved into the daily life of a lower-level minor league baseball team.

The most creative idea came from the Pensacola Blue Wahoos, a Minnesota Twins affiliate, who rented out their ballpark as an Airbnb. Co-owned by professional golfer Bubba Watson, fans could spend the night at the Blue Wahoos Stadium and even play some baseball on the field. The cost was $1,500 for ten guests, which is not a bad price. All 33 dates quickly sold out. The ballpark is located right along Pensacola Bay.

Since no baseball was being played, I saw on Twitter that the Reading Fightin Phils were offering the chance for fans to have a catch on their ballfield for Father's Day on June 21st. The team was going to open their food court and provide live music as well. With the Major League Baseball owners and the Major League Baseball Players Association still not deciding on financial compensation, I thought this might be the only opportunity to visit a ballpark. Plus, with Ian's Little League postponed indefinitely, having a baseball catch on the field of FirstEnergy Stadium might cheer him up. For only $5 per person, I quickly bought two tickets online before the event sold out.

Baseball and Father's Day has always had a special meaning for fans in the Greater Philadelphia area. Most remember Jim Bunning throwing a perfect game on Father's Day on June 21, 1964, at Shea Stadium for older Phillies fans. At the time, Bunning was a father of seven when he retired all 27 Mets on just 90 pitches. On that hot day, more than 32,000 fans witnessed Bunning's perfection. It was a long time that a pitcher in the National League had tossed a perfect game. Unfortunately, the Phillies season ended less than perfect. For Phillies fans, the 1964 season is more remembered for the team's epic collapse down the stretch.

Bunning went on to have a remarkable career. Not only was he elected to the Baseball Hall of Fame, but he was also elected to the U.S. Senate in Kentucky. He served two terms and then decided not to seek reelection. Bunning was only a handful of pitchers to win 100 games in each league. He joined the company of such elite pitchers as Gaylord Perry, Nolan Ryan, and Cy Young. He retired with a record of 224–184 with an ERA of 3.27 throughout his career. Bunning died in 2017 at 85 years of age.

Another great Father's Day baseball moment involved a 500th hit home run at Busch Stadium in St. Louis. On June 20, 2004, Ken Griffey Jr. was at 499 home runs before the game. With his father in the crowd, the Cincinnati Reds start belted home run 500 off Matt Morris in the 6th inning. More than 46,000 fans stood and cheered Griffey even though he was on the opposing team. Griffey Jr. is one of the greatest players in the history of the game. He is always remembered for the level of enthusiasm he brought to the ballpark. The Griffey father and son combination is one of the best in Major League Baseball. Griffey Sr. had played 19 seasons in the majors, including several years with the Reds. "The Kid" retired in 2010 and finished his career with 630 home runs.

With some great Father's Day baseball memories, I was hoping to create some of my own on June 21, 2020. Reading is often referred to as "Baseballtown." The city has had a minor league team going back to 1875 with a team called the Actives. The chance to play on the same field as some former great Phillies ballplayers on Father's Day would be fun. The list reads like a who's who of former Phillies: Larry Bowa (1967-68), Greg Luzinski (1970), Mike Schmidt (1971), Darren Daulton (1983), Juan Samuel (1983), Pat Burrell (1999 and Eastern League Rookie of the Year), Ryan Howard (2004), and Rhys Hoskins (2016 and Eastern League Rookie of the Year). The team's future success runs through Reading.

Before becoming a Phillies minor league affiliate, Reading had some great players from other ball clubs. Rocky Colavito was signed as a teenager by the Cleveland Indians in 1951. He quickly worked his way up through Cleveland's minor league system. He made his debut with Reading in 1953. This was not only important for his baseball career, but Colavito also met his future wife while in Reading. He married Carmen Perrotti in 1954, who lived in a town nearby. He played a handful of games for the Indians in 1955 before making his full debut the next year.

Colavito's baseball career took off once he became an everyday player. He was runner-up for Rookie of the Year in 1956. In 1958 he smashed 42 home runs and was third in the MVP voting. He was loved by the Cleveland fans, signed autographs, and posted great numbers every year. And inexplicably, the Indians owner traded him to the Detroit Tigers. This gave way to the "Curse of Colavito," as the Cleveland organization would go on a bit of a downward slide. Colavito would end up playing for several different teams before retiring in 1968. He finished his career with 374 home runs and was a 9x All-Star. He still lives in the Reading area, although he has had several health problems in recent years.

In the early part of his professional career, Roger Maris also spent time in Reading. Maris began his professional career in 1953 in the Northern League. Like Colavito, Maris was also with the Cleveland Indians organization. He showed early signs of power at the plate, and he quickly moved up the organization. Maris played for the Reading Indians in 1955.

Maris made his Major League debut in 1957 with Cleveland. During the 1958 season, the Indians traded him to the Kansas City Athletics. The rumor has always been that the Kansas City Athletics were almost like a farm team for the New York Yankees. The two teams made numerous trades throughout the years. Maris would end up with the Yankees for the 1960 season. Of course, Maris made history the next year by hitting 61 home runs and breaking Babe Ruth's season record. Despite the home runs, Maris was never as popular as his teammate Mickey Mantle. The stress of 1961 wore on Maris as he approached Ruth's record. He would end up with a decent career and won three World Series titles. The first two were with the Yankees, and his last one was with the St. Louis Cardinals in 1967. He hit .385 in the 1967 World Series. Maris retired after the 1968 season.

In addition to developing future baseball greats, Reading is also known for its pretzels. Although for the early part of its pretzel history, they were spelled "bretzels." In the 19th century, a baker named Benjamin Lichtenthaler was producing more than a million pretzels a year. At one point in the mid-20th Century, Reading's bakeries produced about one-third of the pretzels in the United States. To honor its pretzel past, the Fightin Phils played a few games during the 2019 season as the Reading Pretzels. The team wore a unique pretzel-inspired logo on their hats.

The Fightin Phils are among the few minor league teams that keep part of its MLB organization's name. Reading did undergo a bit of an image overhaul in 2012. It changed its name from Reading Phillies to The Fightin Phils (or the even shorter Fightins), much to the disapproval of its fan base. Over the years, teams have become creative in naming their teams to sell t-shirts and hats. Some of the more interesting names include the Richmond Flying Squirrels, Albuquerque Isotopes (as a nod to *The Simpsons*), Fort Wayne TinCaps (in honor of Johnny Appleseed), and the New Orleans Baby Cakes (although the team is planning to relocate and may change its name). Even nearby Lehigh Valley went with the clever Iron Pigs.

What is up with the ostrich?

As part of the re-branding with the name change in 2012, the team also tinkered with its logo. At the ballpark, a popular hot dog vendor Matt Jackson wore a costume that makes it look like he is riding an ostrich. The team previously used the cursive letter "R" as its primary logo. When the team introduced a cartoonish ostrich with its wings raised as fists, many baseball purists were upset. This was an obvious attempt by the team's marketing department to connect with its younger fan base. In addition to the ostrich logo, the team also slightly altered the color scheme for its uniforms. After 46 years, Reading went for something a little different for the 2013 season.

My personal experience with minor league baseball began in 2001 when Camden, New Jersey, built a ballpark and established a team. The Riversharks were an independent team in the Atlantic League. The team played at Campbell's Field along the Delaware River from 2001 to 2015. The ballpark was tucked under the Ben Franklin Bridge and had a wonderful view of the Philadelphia skyline. Unfortunately, like a lot of independent baseball teams, the Riversharks had difficulty maintaining a fan base. Since the team was not a farm team, no future stars worked their way up through the ranks. Most of the players were not quite ready to give up on their dream of playing professional baseball. The Riversharks did have a few former-MLB players over the years, including Wilson Valdez and Pedro Feliz.

The only time I caught a foul ball at a professional game was at a Riversharks game. The game was nearing the end, and most of the fans had cleared out. I was with Ian, who was probably around five or six at the time. He wanted me to try and get a foul ball, so we moved up toward the concourse area. I had just missed one earlier in the game. If I hustled, I could have probably grabbed it. I would have had to have knocked down this grandfather who was in my way, though. I did not have the heart to knock him over to chase a foul ball at an independent minor league game. With a left-handed batter up, we stationed ourselves along the third base line. The batter took a late swing, and the ball headed our way. The ball quickly moved our way. Luckily, I reached my bare hands out and somehow held onto the baseball. I turned and gave it to Ian, who was smiling. He could not believe I caught it. I could not believe it either. We still have the ball as a souvenir.

I was looking forward to having a catch with Ian on the field of FirstEnergy Stadium. Father's Day is sort of a forgotten holiday hiding in the shadow of Mother's Day. Father's Day was first celebrated on June 19, 1910, in Spokane, Washington. The story goes that Sonora Dodd wanted to honor her dad, a single parent of her and her siblings. Dodd organized an event at the local YMCA, which eventually caught on throughout the United States.

Mother's Day goes back to the Civil War era and was first recognized in West Virginia. Celebrating mothers with flowers or brunch or whatever seems more in line with the spirit of the holiday. It is estimated that Americans spend upwards of $20 billion to honor mom every second Sunday of May. Father's Day just never quite took off in the same way. For myself, becoming a father is the best thing that ever happened to me. All three of my children bring me a lot of happiness. Each child has his or her unique personality, but I love them all equally.

On the morning of June 21st, we started the trip to Reading after eating some breakfast. We packed our baseball gloves, a baseball, and some water. It was a hot and humid day with clear blue skies. In normal times, it would be a perfect day to go and watch a baseball game. I mapped out the trip and figured it should only take about 90 minutes to reach Reading. Traffic was light as we crossed the Walt Whitman Bridge and headed west.

Reading is a city that is trying to rebound to its past glory. Once home to numerous factories, its population was above 100,000 from 1910 to 1950. Its population then went into a decline as factories closed and jobs became scarce. In 2011 the New York Times dubbed Reading as the poorest city in America. It was ahead of cities such as Camden, New Jersey, Gary, Indiana, and Flint, Michigan. Since 2000 though its population has been creeping back upward. Carpenter Technology is a longtime employer in the city. The Santander Arena opened in 2001 and hosts concerts and a minor ice hockey team. The Reading Royals play in the ECHL. The Reading Symphony Orchestra also calls the city home. The city's unemployment rate has gone down in recent years as some jobs have returned. What is sad about the baseball shutdown is that many people depend upon the Fightin Phils for jobs during the summer months. Baseball is more than just the players but also includes the ticket sales, ushers, food vendors, marketing department, and so many other people behind the scenes.

Reading is on the cusp of being in Central Pennsylvania. I mention this because I saw some of the famous Sheetz convenience stores located throughout the area. The debate amongst those in the Philadelphia/New Jersey versus those in the central and western parts of Pennsylvania is which is better: Sheetz or Wawa? Sheetz has its headquarters in Altoona. I do not want to join in the argument as to which one is best. However, both stores seem to have their loyal following. The Pennsylvania Lt. Governor John Fetterman often expresses his preference for Sheetz over Wawa on Twitter. I visited Sheetz for the first time in Reading. I only bought some sodas so I cannot give an honest opinion about which one offers more to its customers.

The drive to Reading was mostly highway. We did not pass through any type of scenic mountains, cascading waterfalls, or flowing rivers. If anyone has ever traveled the Pennsylvania Turnpike, the ride gets boring after the first two or three miles. Each rest top looks the same. I had never been to FirstEnergy Stadium, and it was not hard to find. The stadium, located in an industrial park, is not far from the Schuylkill River. It is easy to see how Reading was once a booming industry town.

People were just pulling up for the 11 A.M. start time. The parking lots were not full, so we pulled right into a spot. Fans were decked out in their red Phillies gear, carried their baseball gloves, and wore their face coverings. The rules were to wear them through the gate, but then it was optional. Every single person I encountered was respectful of maintaining physical distancing and wearing a face covering.

Ian and I checked and walked through the entrance. It was not too crowded since the team capped the tickets at 250 people. Families streamed in and took in the feeling of being back inside a ballpark for the first time this year. A few of the regulars greeted the employees. One could tell that many people were season ticket holders or attended several games per year. This proves the point how minor league teams are a large part of the community. We even saw the local news WFMZ-TV covering the event. Reporter Irene Snyder interviewed a few families as they played catch on the field.

This was the first time I was ever on a professional baseball field. I took a tour of Citizens Bank Park once, but they would not permit visitors even to touch the grass, let alone walk on it. I was amazed at how perfect the grass was on the field. It was like walking on a soft green carpet. My son's Little League fields are filled with rocks, divots and usually have a slope somewhere in the outfield. This was different.

"That kid has a great mullet," Ian said, noticing a boy about ten years old. "He is all business up front but a party in the back."

Sure enough, this 10-year-old kid looked like a miniature version of Kenny Powers from *Eastbound and Down* or a member of the 1993 Phillies team. If his baseball skills match the perfection of his mullet, I can envision this kid being the next John Kruk in about 15 years.

Ian and I headed to the outfield, which had the most space. Like in the movie *Field of Dreams,* fathers and sons (and quite a few daughters) enjoyed the sunshine, blue skies and had a catch at the ballpark. It was just nice to be outside after the longest winters (and a just as long spring). The electronic billboard flashed a "Happy Father's Day" message, and music was piped in through the sound system. We threw the ball back and forth for about 20 minutes or so and soaked up the positive energy.

The temperature was steadily rising, so we headed for some shade. We found a table in the concourse area. Ian had a Pepsi and some French fries. I enjoyed a cold Labatt Blue. At only $6 for a bottle, it seemed like a bargain compared to the price of beers at MLB games. A guy playing guitar was taking requests. Of course, one of the first songs he played was John Fogerty's "Centerfield." The atmosphere was relaxed as people talked about everything but politics and the coronavirus. I think everyone needed a break. I took a few photos of some of the murals around FirstEnergy Stadium. The ballpark has quite a history.

Once the musician started playing "Hotel California" by the Eagles, I figured it was a good time to leave. The temperature was up near 90 degrees, and we already checked out the ballpark. I would like to come back and see a game. The ballpark had a classic feel to it. There did not seem to be a bad seat throughout FirstEnergy Stadium. Minor league baseball has a more intimate feel to it than the big leagues. Everything just seems more accessible to the fans. I took a few last photos, and we headed back to the car.

When Ian and I returned home, we sat on the back porch with the rest of the family. It was the first time in a few weeks that everyone was together. Normally, my daughters are either at work or with their boyfriends. Spending a Sunday afternoon with my children and talking about life should not be taken for granted. I missed the days when the kids were little. We enjoyed each other's company and relaxed in the backyard. I had a beer or three and reflected on life. Delia is in college at Rutgers University, Sophia is doing well in high school and has her first job, and Ian does well in school and wants to run for office one day. All three have bright futures ahead of them. We do not know what tomorrow will bring; however, we were able to enjoy the moment. Much like Jim Bunning's performance on Father's Day in 1964, it turned out to be a perfect day.

6

LOLLYGAGGING IN NORTH CAROLINA

JULY 22–26, 2020

My kids are lollygaggers.

It takes forever to get them moving. When planning on going some-where, they will stare at their phones for an hour before getting out of bed. My son will not start packing until we are ready to go. As bench coach Larry in *Bull Durham* stated to his players, this would make them "lol-lygaggers." Talking about going on vacation is no different. My daughters will complain that the vacation is going to be boring. The destination does not even matter. They anticipate the trip will be dull. And if I mention we are going to visit some museums? Forget about it. Our vacation for the summer of 2020 took some maneuvering on my part. It was no easy task. We settled on North Carolina for the end of July.

At the beginning of the movie *Bull Durham*, Susan Sarandon's character Annie gives a monologue about her belief in baseball. She tried other religions, but it was the only baseball that rung true. Finally, she touches upon some of the principles involving the church of baseball. It is a great opening scene to one of the best sports movies ever. Except for the part about the joy of sleeping with ballplayers, I have to say I agree with most of what Annie believed in.

Durham is primarily known for three things: tobacco, college basketball, and the Durham Bulls. The primary reason for our visit in the summer of 2020 was to see some minor league baseball at Durham Bulls Athletic Park. Professional baseball has been played in Durham since 1902 with the Piedmont League. The Bulls are probably the most famous minor league team, thanks to the *Bull Durham*. Ron Shelton, who wrote and directed the film, played minor league baseball in the late 1960s. Shelton spent time in the Appalachian League and met some memorable characters along the way. The story of Crash Davis (Kevin Costner) taking the young Nuke LaLoosh (Tim Robbins) under his wing is both funny yet telling. Laloosh was loosely based on real-life minor league pitcher Steve Dalkowski. One can only imagine a veteran catcher having similar conversations with a rookie pitcher. Made on a budget of about $9 million, *Bull Durham* would gross more than $50 million in North American. Not exactly *Star Wars* money, but the film was a commercial success.

The film came out in 1988 and put minor league baseball back on the American public radar. Since Bull Durham made its debut, attendance at minor league ballparks has nearly doubled in the last 30 years. The Bulls are usually ranked as one of the highest-valued minor league organizations. The Bulls no longer use the original ballpark used for the film. The team moved to a new ballpark for the 1995 season. At their new ballpark, the Bulls routinely draw more than 500,000 fans a season. Not bad for a team once purchased for $2,400 in 1979. From an attendance perspective, the Miami Marlins drew 811,104 fans in 2018.

In the spirit of *Bull Durham*, the idea to lollygag around North Carolina for a vacation had popped into my head. The state has beaches, baseball, mountains, universities, a diverse restaurant scene, and plenty of state parks. North Carolina had a little something for everyone in my family. It is tough to please three kids with distinct personalities.

Besides Durham, the Tar Heel State provides some other rather historic baseball sites to visit. Babe Ruth hit his first home run as a professional in Fayetteville, North Carolina as a member of the Baltimore Orioles in 1914. The Orioles played a spring training exhibition game when the young Ruth hit a monstrous home run at the Cape Fear Fair Ground. Supposedly, he also acquired the nickname "Babe" from his teammates while in Fayetteville. Before the year was up, his contract would be purchased by the Boston Red Sox. The Babe was well on his way to a Hall of Fame career.

An athlete almost as famous as Ruth also hit a home run in Fayetteville a few years prior. Olympian Jim Thorpe played baseball in the Eastern Carolina League during the summers of 1909–1910. Thorpe attended the Carlisle Indian Industrial School in Pennsylvania. During the summers, he headed south to earn some extra money playing semi-professional baseball. He was more known as a football player and competing in the Olympics, but Thorpe was a decent baseball player. He would have his Olympic medals stripped after it came to light that he played professional baseball in North Carolina. Jim Thorpe was the Bo Jackson in the early 20th Century. His Olympic medals were reinstated to Thorpe in 1983.

I had never spent time in North Carolina. My family and I have driven through on our way to Disney World. In the northeastern part of North Carolina and just across the Virginia border, Murfreesboro is only a six-hour drive from my home in South Jersey. I have known a few people who had enough of New Jersey and moved to Charlotte over the years. As far as I know, they have not looked back since making a move. The time seemed perfect for a trip down I-95 and to experience some southern culture.

My initial plan for a summer vacation was to visit the Field of Dreams Movie Site in Dyersville, Iowa. Also starring Kevin Costner, *Field of Dreams* is probably my own personal favorite sports movie. I have always wanted to take the trip to walk through the corn and have a catch on the Iowa baseball field. Plus. I thought we could cruise along the Mississippi River. However, my children were not thrilled about driving 14 hours to Iowa to visit a baseball diamond in a cornfield or sail along the Mississippi. I admit it was a tough sell. My 16-year-old daughter Sophia let her lack of enthusiasm be known.

"We're going to Iowa for vacation," I suggested one morning.

"I'm not going."

"Why not?"

"Most kids go to Disney or the beach or an island. I'm not going to see a cornfield."

"What if we also visit the World's Largest Truck Stop I-80 in Walcott, Iowa?"

"No."

End of discussion.

We compromised, and the plans were changed to North Carolina with our first stop to the Outer Banks for a few days. So many people rave about visiting the Outer Banks, but I had never made the trip. Towns with names such as Kill Devil Hills, Ocracoke, and Nags Head always held a certain allure with me. The main thing I hear about the beaches in North Carolina is that people can relax and enjoy themselves without the hassle. In New Jersey, we get harassed for beach tags, for playing ball near the water, whistled in by lifeguards if you go deeper than your ankles . . .

After the Outer Banks, the plan was to see some Durham Bulls baseball games. However, as the Major League Baseball owners and players dickered back and forth over money and the pandemic, the minor leagues suffered as a result. On June 30, 2020, the official announcement was made that Minor League Baseball was canceled for the year. The affiliated minor league teams depend on the MLB for their players. As the NBA and NHL planned on re-starting their season, baseball came across as tone-deaf to the real struggles taking place in our country. To have baseball start again on July 4th would have been amazing. Even with no fans in ballparks, it was a chance for the MLB to recapture some of its past glory. We continued with the planning of our trip to North Carolina.

Life is funny but not always. I love the game of baseball. It is a distraction. I often become annoyed when people are untrue to themselves. Some may use the phrase "keeping it real" or some type of cliché. My wife and I would argue for a week straight. Then when we would hang out with her family or friends, she would make it seem like everything was cool. It is crazy. I would become detached. I could not go through the motions of pretending "everything was cool" between us. Maybe that makes me a lesser person.

However, I use my passion for baseball almost as an emotional crutch. The ebb and flow of a game take my mind off things. The strange part is that I normally care less about who wins the game. I just like the sense of enjoying the game. Baseball fills the void. I am thankful for my job, co-workers, friends, and family, yet I feel unsatisfied. I have three healthy kids. My brother has a little boy that I want to watch grow up. I have much to be thankful for, yet my life is incomplete. What have I accomplished? I feel like a nothing. But when I take my kids to Citizens Bank Park or some minor league park, I feel like we are sharing something special. It is difficult to explain.

Planning a summer vacation around some baseball is a way of connecting with my family. Sara and our oldest daughter already had a trip planned to Europe (this was eventually canceled). So, instead of taking in the culture in Prague or wherever, my two younger children and I would be in the Outer Banks and then on to Durham. You could call it our mini-tour of the south. Plus, it would give us another excuse to visit a Waffle House for eggs, grits, and waffles. The coffee is always hot, the price is right, and the food is edible.

The Outer Banks was appealing to me. I like being near the ocean. During the winter months, I often will take a ride to the Jersey Shore. I only live about 45 minutes or so from Atlantic City. I like staring into the ocean, smelling the salt air, and hearing the squawk of seagulls. I find it reassuring and cleansing at the same time. I would like to say it is a time to reflect by staring into the greenish hue of the Atlantic Ocean; however, I am not a real deep thinker. I like to be distracted. It is easier on the soul. I often regret the mistakes of my past. Sometimes I wish I could just turn the page and move on.

In keeping with a baseball theme, I wanted to purchase tickets for the Durham Bulls ahead of time. Once the coronavirus hit, though, those plans went awry like a wild pitch hitting up against the backstop. Baseball is quite popular in North Carolina. Durham has an especially rich history. Their alumni include Joe Morgan, Andruw Jones, Chipper Jones, Kevin Millwood, Scott Kazmir, James Shields, and Ben Zobrist have all spent time in North Carolina. Unfortunately, Minor League Baseball's future is on thin ice. Despite 41.5 million fans attending a minor league game in 2019, teams get little support from Major League Baseball. Despite the strong ties to local communities, MLB has been in talks to eliminate about 40 teams throughout the minor league ranks. Throw in the COVID-19 pandemic and the economic meltdown, and most minor league organizations are now struggling financially.

Baseball in North Carolina goes back to the early 1900s. Winston-Salem has had a professional minor league since 1905. Despite a brief interruption during the Great Depression and again during WW II, a team has been consistently playing in Winston-Salem since the inception of the Carolina League in 1945. The team was initially called the Twins, not after Minnesota but rather the twin cities of Winston and Salem before merging into one.

In the early to mid part of the 20th Century, the Textile Leagues were popular in North Carolina and South Carolina. These leagues centered around the textile industry, with each town fielding its baseball team. Baseball provided the small mill towns with an opportunity to get behind their home team and give the community a sense of pride. The larger textile factories provided company housing, social events, a company store, and some even schooling for the employees' children. Baseball soon became an integral part of the textile mill industry.

The organized mill leagues popping up throughout the Carolinas were extremely competitive. The Greenville Cotton Mill Base Ball

League was established in 1907. The Piedmont League soon followed this in 1912. Many games would draw crowds of 1,500 to watch some baseball. It was not until the 1950s when the textile mill leagues began to wane in popularity. With the rise of automobiles and television, the American public turned its attention elsewhere. Nevertheless, the Carolinas produced many great players from the textile mill leagues. The first star player was Champ Osteen from a Piedmont team. He played for many different teams for more than two decades.

The most famous baseball player who emerged from the Textile Leagues is Shoeless Joe Jackson. Born in Pickens County, South Carolina, Jackson went to work in the cotton mills as a child. At the age of seven or eight, he was already working 12-hour shifts as a "lint head" in the textile mills. Then, as a teenager, he began playing for the different textile mill leagues. His baseball reputation quickly spread throughout the Carolinas.

Jackson first broke in Major League Baseball with the Philadelphia Athletics. Playing in a large city, though, was overwhelming for him. On a few different occasions, Jackson jumped the team for a team and headed back home. The Philadelphia fans taunted Jackson for his country ways and for not being able to read. Baseball in the early 1900s had few Southerners. His teammates teased even Ty Cobb. Eventually, his reluctance to play in Philadelphia forced Connie Mack to send him to the Cleveland Naps for the 1910 season. By 1911, he was hitting .408 for the Naps (yet not leading the American League!) and found his comfort zone.

Although illiterate, Jackson was smart when it came to his finances. He wanted more money than Cleveland was willing to pay him. During the 1915 season, Jackson was traded to the Chicago White Sox. During his time with the White Sox, he was in the prime of his career. His batting average was .341 for the 1916 season. It was also with the White Sox when Jackson became involved with fixing the 1919 World Series. The story has been told a thousand times before, but it should be noted that Shoeless Joe was caught up in the fix. During the early part of the 20th Century, gambling on baseball was rampant. The White Sox and their owner Charles Comiskey often disagreed over salaries and bonuses. Despite batting .375 during the World Series, collecting 12 hits, and hitting the only home run, Jackson was implicated in throwing games along with a few of his teammates.

Jackson's last season in Major League Baseball was 1920. Although he was not found guilty in a court of law, he was barred from playing baseball by Commissioner Kenesaw Mountain Landis. Jackson played on different semi-professional teams for several years in the South. His career playing at an elite level was over at 32 years of age. In his final season with the White Sox, he batted .382 for the season. Jackson claimed innocence in being a part of fixing the World Series. His performance during the World Series is still debated to this day.

After his banishment from baseball, Jackson and his wife ran various businesses in Greenville. Joe Jackson's Liquor Store operated until he died in 1951. Today Greenville, South Carolina, is home to the Shoeless Joe Jackson Museum. His lifetime career batting average was .356, which ranks third on the all-time list.

In 1943 a "non-professional" team playing baseball in Chapel Hill, North Carolina, featured some of the day's biggest stars. The Chapel Hill Cloud Busters, a team, made up of enlisted Navy cadets, featured Ted Williams, his Boston Red Sox teammate Johnny Pesky, Johnny Sain of the Boston Braves. Williams and many of his fellow ballplayers were training to be fighter pilots at the University of North Carolina. The university hosted the cadets for classroom work and physical training while providing its normal academic semester for its students. The Cloud Busters practiced and played games at Emerson Field.

North Carolina has a link to a baseball term that many believe to be true. I have read different articles on the subject, but I am unsure where I stand on believing the story. The term "bullpen" allegedly refers to the huge Bull Durham tobacco signs (in the shape of a bull) in numerous minor league ballparks in the early 1900s. During the summer heat, the relief pitchers would be seeking relief in the shade of the giant bull-shaped advertisement on the outfield wall. When the manager needed a new pitcher, the call was made to the "bullpen." The only problem is the term was used before the Bull Durham tobacco advertisements. It makes for a good story, but I am not certain it is entirely true.

One thing that is true: The North Carolina Baseball Museum resides in the town of Wilson, North Carolina, and is just a few miles off I-95. The museum is housed in historic Fleming Stadium and staffed entirely by volunteers. It features plenty of memorabilia and highlights the players from North Carolina elected to the Baseball Hall of Fame. Fleming Stadium opened in 1939 and is home to the Wilson Tobs (short for Tobacconists). The Tobs play in the Coastal Plain League, which is a summer league that showcases college players.

The Coastal Plain League is currently made up of more than a dozen teams from Georgia, North Carolina, South Carolina, and Virginia. The original league had its start in the 1930s but then had to halt during WW II. The original Coastal Plain League started up again in 1946 and lasted a few more seasons. The current version of the league has been around since the 1990s and plays a 52-game schedule beginning at the end of May. Players such as Justin Verlander and Ryan Zimmerman played a summer in the Coastal Plain League before finding success in Major League Baseball. Another player known more for football than baseball who also played a summer was Russel Wilson. He ended up choosing football over baseball and won Super Bowl with the Seattle Seahawks. I kept checking the Facebook page of the Wilson Tobs; however, all indications showed they were playing but not in front of fans.

North Carolina features an additional summer league for college baseball players. The Tidewater Summer League was established in 1946 in Norfolk, Virginia. It is one of the oldest "wood bat" collegiate baseball leagues in the United States. This is a showcase type of league that allows college players to get some additional looks from baseball scouts. Similar leagues include the Cape Cod Baseball League and the Alaska Baseball League. These amateur leagues allow players to play additional games while keeping their NCAA eligibility.

I was hoping to see the Outer Banks Daredevils play during our trip. However, due to COVID-19, the organization decided not to field a team in 2020. As a result, the Tidewater Summer League, was played in

2020 with only four teams: Edenton Steamers, Greenbrier Knights, Old Dominion Hitters, and the Tidewater Drillers. Much like the Coastal Plain League, many teams opted out of the 2020 season. Nevertheless, the Tidewater Summer League has produced some great MLB players throughout its history. Some of their famous alumni include Ryan Zimmerman, Melvin Upton Jr., and Michael Cuddyer.

It seems that I struck out with the Durham Bulls, Wilson Tobs, and even the Outer Banks Daredevils. Unfortunately, I was not going to have the opportunity to see any future stars play. These summer leagues provide such an intimate environment to watch a ball game. Even the Alaska Baseball League postponed playing until 2021. I was disappointed it was not going to work out to see any baseball for our summer trip. Maybe I can start planning a visit to Alaska with the kids to watch baseball up near the Arctic Circle. It may be difficult to convince the kids to take a 4,300-mile car trip to watch the Chugiak Chinooks play the Anchorage Bucs.

Some other great players have come from North Carolina. These MLB players include Smoky Burgess, Jim Bibby, Buck Leonard, and Enos Slaughter. However, one of my favorite players (non-Phillies) is Madison Bumgarner. Also known as secret rodeo champion Mason Saunders, Bumgarner is a three-time World Series Champion who owns a 100-acre farm in Lenoir, North Carolina. He pitches with intensity and passion but also knows how to ride a horse. He is the one player (okay, maybe Mike Trout) that I wish to play for my Phillies.

One player I never fully appreciated is Jim "Catfish" Hunter. He played just a few years before I started following baseball. I caught the tail end of his career. As I started researching for this book, his career numbers and World Series rings blew me away. Hunter won three World Series Championships with the Oakland Athletics and two with the New York Yankees. He pitched a perfect game in 1968 against the Minnesota Twins. Hunter was from Hertford, North Carolina, and returned to his farm there after retiring from baseball. He developed arm troubles while in his early 30s and retired from baseball at 33 years of age. He is often referred to as one of the nicest players in Major League Baseball by all accounts. He had a down-to-earth manner and friendly nature. Sadly, he died from ALS in 1999. He was only 53 years old.

One of the true characters of baseball is from Williamston, North Carolina. Gaylord Perry and his brother Jim both had long careers within Major League Baseball. They only trail Joe and Phil Niekro for most wins in baseball for brothers. The Perry brothers have a fascinating background, and, amazingly, both reached the big leagues. They grew up with little money on a farm with their parents and a younger sister. Their father was a sharecropper who tried to scratch out a living growing tobacco. Gaylord and his brother helped by working on the farm six days a week and tried to fit in baseball when they had a chance. Their father, Evan, was something of a baseball player himself.

Gaylord would end up winning more than 300 games over a 22-year career. He won the Cy Young Award twice (one in the American League and one in the National League) and was elected to the Baseball Hall of Fame in 1991. He did not have overpowering stuff as a pitcher, but he learned the spitball from Bob Shaw in 1964 and used it to his advantage. Gaylord perfected the pitch and even named his autobiography *Me and the Spitter*. His fiddling on the mound was sometimes more of a distraction to the batter than the actual pitch. Touching his hair, nose, cap, pants, the rosin bag, and whatever else, Gaylord turned it into an art form. He ended up pitching in 777 games in Major League Baseball. Many seasons he pitched more than 300 innings. He was a true workhorse as a player. Not a bad career for the son of a tobacco farmer from Eastern North Carolina. It should be noted, he also tossed a no-hitter against Bob Gibson and the Cardinals in 1968.

The closest I ever came to witness a no-hitter involved a pitcher from North Carolina. Kevin Millwood tossed a no-hitter on April 27, 2003, against the San Francisco Giants. I was on my way to Veterans Stadium that day with my daughter Delia who was not quite four years old. We were crossing the Walt Whitman Bridge when I realized the circus was at the Spectrum, across the street from the Phillies' stadium. We ended up going to see clowns, elephants, and the greatest show on Earth. I missed the no-hitter because I was across the street.

Kevin Millwood was born in Gastonia, North Carolina. He never quite lived up to what he accomplished with the Atlanta Braves during his time in Philadelphia. Millwood was part of a second no-hitter with the Seattle Mariners in 2012. Just for the record, Steve Carlton never threw a no-hitter during his Hall of Fame career. Baseball is a simple game, but it is also a complicated one. Sometimes the numbers do not always add up.

One former All-Star player from North Carolina almost derailed his career before reaching the big leagues. Josh Hamilton, born in Raleigh, was a high school star at Athens Drive High School. He excelled both as an outfielder and pitcher. The Tampa Bay Rays selected him with the first pick in the 1999 MLB Draft. While in their minor league system, Hamilton began using drugs. He struggled for many years before overcoming his demons. Eventually, he became an All-Star with the Texas Rangers. He wrote about his struggles, faith, and baseball career in his book *Beyond Belief: Finding the Strength to Come Back.*

North Carolina has never had an MLB team; however, the state hosted an official game at Fort Bragg in 2016. The Miami Marlins defeated the Atlanta Braves by a score of 5–2 in front of a crowd of more than 12,000 military members and their families. J.T. Realmuto of the Marlins hit the only home run. This was the first time an MLB game was played on an active military base. The ballpark was built in just a few months to accommodate this historic game. ESPN did the broadcast of the game for their *Sunday Night Baseball.*

North Carolina currently has 11 minor league teams from the Asheville Tourists to the Winston-Salem Dash. The team with the best name is either the Hickory Crawdads or the Carolina Mudcats. North Carolina may be more famous for its college basketball teams and the early days of stock car racing; however, there is plenty of baseball being played throughout the state. Teams have usually been associated with either the South Atlantic League or the Western Carolinas League. The team is an affiliate of the Washington Senators. One interesting bit of baseball trivia is that Babe Ruth's first professional home run was hit in Fayetteville,

North Carolina, in 1914. He was a newly signed player of the Baltimore Orioles (not affiliated with the current team) at the time.

A long-time family friend, Albert Richards, played briefly for the Shelby Senators during the 1969 season. In addition to Shelby, he also played in Salisbury, North Carolina. Over the years, he has told me numerous stories about his days playing for the Washington Senators minor league organization. Richards once showed me a photo of when Ted Williams (then the Senators) manager visited his minor league team in spring training. Many of his stories involve long bus rides, though, while playing in the Western Carolinas League. He always speaks fondly though of his time playing baseball.

In addition to seeing some baseball, I wanted to see the Wright Brothers National Memorial at Kill Devil Hills. Orville and Wilbur Wright first took a flight of significant length along the beaches of North Carolina on December 17, 1903. At the time, Babe Ruth was just a kid in Baltimore stealing fruit, chewing tobacco, and deemed "incorrigible" by his parents. However, the Wright brothers were not as mischievous as the young Ruth. Whereas the Babe's father ran a saloon, their father was a bishop in the Church of the United Brethren in Christ. In their bicycle shop in Ohio, Orville and Wilbur liked tinkering with mechanical projects specializing in aviation. They decided on the Outer Banks because of the strong winds and the wide-open area along the beaches.

Their story is just as much the American dream as Babe Ruth's. In 1909 President William Howard Taft awarded the Wright brothers Aero Club of America medals at the White House. Orville and Wilbur went from tinkering with flight designs and gliders at their family home to eventually visiting Europe as air travel quickly gained popularity. The brothers would often test their gliders, make some adjustments, and then go back out again. Since we would be in the Outer Banks, a stop at the Wright Brothers Memorial was on our list of places to visit.

In addition to baseball and visiting the Wright Brothers National Memorial, I figured we would hit at least one or two more Waffle Houses during our trip to North Carolina. With close to 200 locations, North

Carolina is second only to George with the number of restaurants. Thus, finding a Waffle House is relatively easy to find in the Tar Heel State.

North Carolina is the largest producer of tobacco in the United States. Kentucky, Tennessee, Virginia, and South Carolina also have quite a few tobacco farms but not as many as North Carolina. Tobacco farming is hard work and not as profitable as it was in years past. Since the 1960s, the number of Americans who smoke has been declining. Tobacco farming, though, is still an important part of the North Carolina state economy. It is a big part of the culture as well. Cigarettes such as Winston and Salem were named after North Carolina cities. Tourists can visit the Tobacco Farm Life Museum in Kenly. The museum is open year-round and highlights the heritage and history of tobacco farming.

North Carolina had a semi-pro baseball league called the Tobacco State League operating from 1946 to 1950. After WW II, people looked to life returning to normal and flocked to baseball games throughout the country. The Tobacco State League contained between six to eight teams during its five-year existence. Hundreds of fans would turn out each night to watch a mix of local heroes, former pro-players, and college ballplayers. Many of the smaller cities showed great pride in their local team. Some legendary players included Hank Nesselrode and Van Lingle Mungo, who had the greatest name in baseball history. Unfortunately, the league dissolved after the 1950 season as attendance fell off.

With COVID-19 ramping back up, unemployment at recession levels, and civil protests throughout the country, it was not an ideal time to take a vacation. However, my younger children needed a break from quarantine, their sports being canceled, and not being able to do normal kid stuff. Plus, the wife and I were trying to reconcile our differences. I had to leave my childhood home and return to the home I was still helping to pay the mortgage. My father was afraid I would catch the coronavirus and pass it on to him. Life was complicated. We reserved a long weekend in the Outer Banks for late July with everything topsy-turvy and nothing quite normal.

While still trying to figure out how to catch a baseball game in North Carolina, I made reservations at the Cape Hatteras Motel in Buxton.

This town is at the southernmost point of the Outer Banks. I figured with the coronavirus still going strong, it was best to stay away from the more heavily populated areas such as Duck, Nag's Head, and Kitty Hawk. The motel was located right on the beach and not far from the Cape Hatteras Lighthouse. Looking at their website, the place seemed like the perfect vacation spot.

On the morning of July 22nd, the car was packed, and we began our journey to the Outer Banks. My oldest daughter Delia had to drive separately with her boyfriend because we could not all fit in the car. In my car was Sara, our daughter Sophia, Ian, and myself. We left the dog behind with a family friend. The whole family would be together again. Before the journey began, my wife gave me an ultimatum.

"You have to promise that you won't dip tobacco and listen to country music on the way down," she said a few days before the trip. She gets grossed out by this habit. I cannot say I blame her. I have tried to quit numerous times. I always seem to go back to it, though.

I reluctantly agreed to the no tobacco or country music terms. Country music would not be a problem. I am not even much of a fan. It just takes my mind off my problems when I am driving. All the songs sound the same to me. Most of the music seems to involve a truck, a broken heart, a bottle of beer, and not necessarily in that order. I cannot tell the difference between Kenny Chesney or Florida Georgia Line, or whoever else.

Giving up tobacco while driving was going to be a bigger problem.

I have a love-hate relationship when it comes to tobacco. Some Skoal longcut tobacco in the lower lip has always been an enjoyable habit. I have been doing it off and on since my college days. I would turn to chewing tobacco when I was giving up smoking cigarettes. I try and quit dipping tobacco, but for some reason always return to it. I have not smoked a cigarette in more than 20 years. I am always worried about getting throat or mouth cancer. Losing your jaw to cancer is something of a buzzkill. And not many people like seeing a person spit into an empty 7-Eleven coffee cup and think, "wow, I'd like to talk to him." A pinch of tobacco, some Mountain Dew, and a full tank of gas. What else does a person need to travel?

Hatteras Island is approximately 400 miles from my home in New Jersey. It was home to the "Graveyard of the Atlantic," with more than 2,000 shipwrecks off its coast. Once again, we headed south on I-95 with the intention of finding a bit of relaxation, taking in nature, enjoying the beach and ocean, and hopefully reconnecting with one another. Like most families, our time is spent either working, running around, or getting lost in the trials and tribulations of daily life. I was hoping we could put our cell phone downs for a few days and simply enjoy life and each other's company.

I reserved a room in Buxton, which is in the southern part of the Outer Banks. At the time, I did not realize it is an hour's drive south from Kill Devil Hills. Looking at Google Maps, it is deceiving how far Hatteras Island is from the area with the attractions. The Cape Hatteras Motel turned out to be in a perfect location, though. It was near a few restaurants, was literally on the beach, within easy access to NC Highway 12 (not much of a highway), had a swimming pool, the people were all friendly, yet it was far enough removed to have some peace and quiet. It was an old-style hotel in a quiet section of the Outer Banks. The last thing I wanted was to have other families setting up their beach umbrellas within arm's reach of where I planned to relax on the beach.

It might have been wishful thinking on my part.

On the ride to North Carolina, we stopped at another Waffle House. I am not even sure of the town where we stopped to eat. I believe it was somewhere near Richmond, Virginia. It was weird to walk in and see some of the diners sitting at their spaced-apart tables. Of course, people must remove their face coverings to eat, but it was still strange. As much as I love their egg and cheese biscuits, I do not want to risk getting the coronavirus to get one. We ordered our food to-go and ate in the parking lot.

The impact of the pandemic seriously affected the business of Waffle Houses throughout the United States. The company had to lay off thousands of its 40,000 workers. Normally, the Waffle House can reopen once a disaster strikes a location. But, with a virus, everything is different. After Hurricane Hugo devastated Charleston, South Carolina, the local

Waffle House opened and fed the emergency workers. Only as governors lifted restrictions has the restaurant been able to invite customers to enjoy their meals inside.

This trip did not turn out as initially planned, but sometimes everything works out in the end. We were not able to see any baseball games or even visit The North Carolina Baseball Museum. We never did walk around the Wright Brothers Memorial in Kitty Hawk. I told the kids we would sand surf at Jockey's Ridge State Park. We did not do that either. None of us felt comfortable with indoor dining. These are strange times we currently live in. Hopefully, as you read this, life has returned to being somewhat more normal. Even with some bumps in the road, all was not lost. Despite the missed opportunities, North Carolina was well worth the visit.

Another nice aspect of the vacation was Major League Baseball officially returned while we were in North Carolina. Ian and I watched a little of the Yankees and Nationals game on ESPN. Despite the constant drudgery of the news and politics, the start of baseball was a bright spot. Dr. Anthony Fauci threw out the first pitch. As Bob Uecker would say, his pitch "was just a bit outside."

I will not go into the details of the vacation. I tend to be a marginal character in this theater called life. The kids played in the surf, parasailed for the first time, we ordered take-out seafood, and we simply enjoyed the sunshine. Ian tried Royal Crown Cola for the first time and loved it. I ended up buying a 12-pack of RC Cola to take home. Sophia had Moon Pies. Delia and her boyfriend did some surf fishing. I liked being able to buy six-packs of beer at gas stations or grocery stores in North Carolina. A person cannot walk into the local Shell station in New Jersey and pick up some Coors Banquet beers while filling their car up with gas. Wherever we went, the Hatteras Lighthouse loomed off in the distance. We were close to the ocean the entire trip. It was so hot, I had to jump into the ocean just to cool off throughout the day. My wife and I ate different types of seafood. I tried some Spanish mackerel which was delicious. For a few days, we simply existed by soaking in the sun, splashing in the surf, and gazing up at the blue skies. We took a break from the gravity of the situation unfolding throughout the United States. I tried to stay off Twitter as well. Our family needed to slowly exhale for even just a few days.

The people of North Carolina are some of the friendliest people I have ever met. Every person was welcoming and said hello. One thing a few people mentioned was the destruction of Hurricane Dorian in 2019. The storm caused some damage to the area. We took a ferry ride to Ocracoke Island. Many homes and businesses were still being repaired from the storm. I have never experienced the power of a hurricane. Dorian caused serious flooding and pounded the foundations of many homes. Dare County celebrated its 150th Anniversary in 2020. The whole area gives off the vibe of being from a slower, more relaxed time. Down in Avon, Buxton, and Hatteras Village, we did not see any chain restaurants. I saw plenty of golden sunrises but not one Golden Arches.

Even the seagulls seemed nicer in North Carolina than in New Jersey. At the Jersey Shore beaches, a seagull will swoop down and snatch a potato chip out of your hand if one is not paying attention. The birds have a Tony Soprano Jersey-type of attitude. Along the beaches of Cape Hatteras, the seagulls searched for their natural foods and gave little notice of much else.

On our first full day in Buxton, I strolled down to the beach before the town woke up. I can never sleep in. Even on vacation, I wake up early. Walking along the water's edge, the beach was mostly deserted except for a few seagulls and ghost crabs. The sun peeked out over the horizon and gave some color to the sky. From our motel room, we could watch the sunrise and the sunset. It was amazing. A person could get used to living in the Outer Banks. It had been a difficult year up to this point, but I had not given up hope. I am not deeply religious, but I try and take notice. It only takes an open heart and open mind. I always forget and get caught up in the daily nonsense. I forget to hit the pause button. Staring out into the Atlantic Ocean, I took a deep breath and appreciated all life had to offer.

The sky displayed a multitude of pink and orangish hues. A few streaky clouds decorated the horizon. The day was just beginning, and the possibilities were endless.

7

OPENING DAY

JULY 23, 2020

Richard Wang will never be confused with Vin Scully.

April 2020 arrived, and I found myself cheering for the Rakuten Monkeys in the Chinese Professional Baseball League (CPBL). Crazier things have happened, I suppose. First, I had to watch baseball from Taiwan via a live Twitter feed. Then, COVID-19 shut down all professional, college, high school, and youth sports throughout the United States. As a result, the opening day of Major League Baseball was put on hold indefinitely. I ended up enjoying Wang, and his partner Wayne Scott McNeil describe the games from Taiwan. They are both knowledgeable of the players, call the action as they see it, and have quirky chemistry. The CPBL is probably on the level of AA-minor league baseball in the United States. However, watching baseball in the spring is something I look forward to every year. By December, I am already counting down the days when players report to spring training.

My son and I have started a tradition of attending the home opener for the Phillies at Citizens Bank Park. It is something we hope to continue to do for as long as we can. Ian told me he would then like to continue the tradition with his kids. I am lucky that he has the same love of baseball. It will be fun to take him and his sons or daughters to a Phillies game as a grandpop. Baseball is about connecting one generation to the next. The game allows parents and their children to share the memories of a favorite player or moment from a game. Ian and I had a chance to meet my favorite player when I was his age.

Pete Rose was appearing at a local card show outside Philadelphia a few years ago. Ian and I had our photo taken with the Hit King. I had to pay (Pete does nothing for free). It is one of my favorite photos. If not for Rose, the Phillies would not have won their first World Series in 1980. Our brief encounter with Rose is a connection Ian will be able to show his children one day. Baseball is all about creating memories. We shook hands with the all-time leader in hits in Major League Baseball. I told Rose that my son plays Little League baseball. His advice was to "hustle because you want to win, right. Winning makes playing the game a lot more fun." He speaks the truth.

On August 22, 2020, Ian and I attended an autograph signing event with another one of my favorite Phillies players. Steve Jeltz played for the Phillies from 1983 to 1989. Born in Paris, Jeltz has the most hits of any MLB player born in France. He was not the greatest player, but I always liked him. He had a sense of style about him even though he never became an All-Star. Jeltz was nice and offered to have my son stand next to him for a photo. He had recently moved from Kansas to Carlisle, Pennsylvania. He assists with a local youth baseball clinic in Central Pennsylvania. Jeltz is a positive role model and talked baseball with us for a few minutes. During a rough year due to the pandemic, meeting him was a true highlight.

I knew my own future as a baseball player was over when I went to bat and noticed "the shift." In Major League Baseball, a shift usually means when a left-handed pull-hitter is up, the third baseman moves to short, and the shortstop will stand on second base. The defense is anticipating the hitter will still pull the ball to the right side of the field. For me, the shift meant the outfield moved up and stood next to the infielders. I was a weak hitter, but this was truly embarrassing. It was the third baseman, left fielder, shortstop, centerfielder, second baseman, right fielder, and first baseman all playing up. I did not have enough pop in my bat to hit the ball over their heads. The gig was up. I "retired" from baseball at 13 years old.

I still loved baseball, though. Even if I could have played in high school, my grades were not good enough. My school career matched my baseball career. Below mediocre. My grades were good enough to attend college; however, I was not getting any offers from Ivy League schools. While at West Chester University, I remember watching the 1993 Phillies on television reach the World Series. This ragtag group of players, including Lenny Dykstra, John Kruk, and Mitch Williams, made watching baseball fun again. Unfortunately, the following year baseball went on strike, and the 1994 World Series did not happen.

It was after college that I started to dig in with the history of the game. I enjoyed reading about the players in the early 20th Century. Then, the game seemed to move at a faster pace. Grover Cleveland Alexander could set the pace of the game and have it finished in under 90 minutes. From 1914 to 1918, Alexander pitched more than 30 complete games, and 300 innings pitched each season. Now, pitchers may not even reach 30 complete games for their career. My love of baseball returned, but I watched the game from a historical perspective. I think I appreciated its history more. Once my children were born, I enjoyed taking them to see the Phillies at Veterans Stadium and then Citizens Bank Park.

For whatever reason, Ian likes to tailgate before the game in the parking lot. I will pack some sodas, beers, and some potato chips. We always bring our gloves and a baseball. We will have a catch until the parking lot fills up with other fans going to the ballgame. Normally I will try and drink a few beers before heading into the game. Drinking beer in the parking lot is cheaper than inside the ballpark. I am not exactly above drinking in a parking lot beneath I-95 before a Phillies game.

The first official Opening Day for the National League took place on April 22, 1876, in Philadelphia. The Boston Red Stockings defeated the Philadelphia Athletics (not the Connie Mack team) 6–5 at Jefferson Street Park. It was reported that a rather large crowd of more than 3,000 fans attended this first game. This is about the average size crowd of a Miami Marlins game. The game lasted about two hours which is less than half the average World Series game. I cannot figure out why the modern game takes more than four hours to complete.

Harry Wright managed the Red Stockings at that time. He coached Boston up until 1881. Wright finished his career managing the Phillies from 1884 to 1893. He died in 1895 and is buried in the West Laurel Hill Cemetery right outside of Philadelphia. A few years ago, my son and I paid a visit to his gravesite so I could take a few photos. Wright is often considered the "Father of Baseball" rather than Doubleday. The statue of Wright at the cemetery shows a rather regal-looking fellow. Ian was bored, so we did not stay long. A 12-year-old kid does not have the same appreciation of baseball's history as his father.

For many, many years, the Cincinnati Reds have been the unofficial team to open the MLB season. Dating back to the 1880s, Opening Day has been something special in Cincinnati. In the early days of the National League, Cincinnati was considered the southernmost city in baseball. The Cincinnati Red Stocks were the first all-professional team in 1869. Frank Bancroft, the business manager of the Reds, saw the season opener as a great business opportunity for the ball club. Thousands of fans came out to watch the Reds for the first game. Often, a standing-room-only crowd could squeeze into League Park. In the late 19th Century, most of the of revenue was generated from ticket sales. Bancroft saw to it that Opening Day became something special.

By the time the Reds moved to Crosley Field, Opening Day had become something of a celebration to the residents of Queen City. The Findlay Market Parade began in 1920. The market was a place to gather for fans to celebrate Opening Day. Over the years, the parade has expanded to even include elephants under the ownership of Marge Schott. The Reds are no longer always the team to start the season; however, the tradition of making it a day to celebrate began in Cincinnati.

The first president to throw out a pitch on opening day was William Howard Taft in 1910 before a Washington Senators and Philadelphia Athletics game. Taft, one of our larger presidents, tossed the ball to Walter Johnson. During the seventh inning, Taft had to stretch his legs. Since the fans saw the president standing between innings, everyone in Griffith Stadium stood as well. Hence, a new tradition was started in baseball. Or at least that is one theory. Since Taft has thrown out the first pitch at Opening Day except Jimmy Carter (although Carter threw out the first pitch before Game 7 of the 1979 World Series), every president has thrown out the first pitch. President Trump has yet to throw out a first pitch (as of this writing).

Opening Day is special regardless of the weather. Ian and I were at the game when Bryce Harper made his debut at Citizens Bank Park in 2019. We were both excited he signed with the Phillies. I thought for sure he would have gone to the Dodgers. Instead, Harper said and did all the right things after signing with Philadelphia. He made people care about baseball again in a football town. In his first year, Harper lived up to expectations. He hit 35 home runs along with 114 RBIs. Plus, he and his wife had their first child. He connected with the fans and did all the right things.

The Phillies have hosted some unusual events on its Opening Day throughout the years. In 1972 the Phillies planned to have Kiteman leap off a ramp in the upper level of Veterans Stadium to deliver the baseball for the first pitch. Bill Giles was the master of off-beat promotions for the Phillies. He held a variety of different positions within the Phillies organization throughout the years. His father, Warren, was involved in Major League Baseball for decades as well. However, the idea of Kiteman was different even for Bill Giles. With a giant kite strapped to his back, Richard Johnson made his way down the ramp only to crash into the upper-level seats and not even making it onto the field. The Philadelphia fans were not impressed.

For the opening of Veterans Stadium in 1971, the Phillies had the ceremonial first ball dropped from a helicopter to their backup catcher. Mike Ryan waited on the field as the helicopter hovered above. Ryan would later recall that there were three options for him that day. He could drop the ball and get booed by the home crowd, catch the ball, or get killed. He made the catch, much to the delight of the fans. Ryan later became a coach for the Phillies and repeated the stunt in 1981, 1991, and 1995.

There have been more successful Opening Days for fans and players throughout the history of baseball. However, the most impressive performance was by Walter Johnson of the Washington Senators in 1926. Known as "The Big Train," Johnson pitched a complete game shutout to defeat the Philadelphia Athletics 1–0. What made this game even more incredible is that the game lasted 15 innings. For 14 Opening Day starts for his career, Johnson had a 1.31 ERA with nine wins.

Another great performance was by a 21-year-old Bob Feller on April 16, 1940. Feller threw the first no-hitter on Opening Day against the Chicago White Sox. The Cleveland Indians hurler was a little wild as he walked five, but he gave up no hits while striking out eight. Despite his youthful age, Feller already had a few seasons under his belt. The future Hall of Famer had burst onto the scene as a 17-year-old in 1936. Unfortunately, he would end up missing three of his prime seasons while serving in WW II. Despite the missed seasons, he is regarded as one of the best pitchers of his generation. To this day, Feller is the only pitcher to toss a no-hitter on Opening Day. A few have come close, but the Heater from Van Meter is still the only one.

April 4, 1974, was an Opening Day of historical note. After waiting all winter, Hank Aaron hit home run number 714 at Riverfront Stadium to tie Babe Ruth's record. The Braves great hit the home run off Reds pitcher Jack Billingham. Throughout the winter, Aaron received death threats and hate mail. Aaron is often overlooked because he was not just a consistent home run hitter, but he was an unbelievable all-around player. Finally, on April 8th, Aaron hit home run number 715 to break Ruth's record. Hammerin' Hank retired with more than 3,700 hits and 755 career home runs. In my eyes, Aaron is still the all-time home run leader.

A more recent Opening Day of significance was the performance by Clayton Kershaw of the Dodgers in 2013. Kershaw not only pitched a complete game shutout, but he also hit his first career home run. To make the victory even sweeter, the Dodgers defeated their hated rival San Francisco Giants at Dodger Stadium. Kershaw would go on to win his second Cy Young Award in 2013. He is one player (non-Phillies player) who I would like to see win a World Series (update: he did in 2020). Before moving to Los Angeles, the Dodgers were responsible for an even more important Opening Day performance.

The most historic Opening Day took place on April 15, 1947, when Jackie Robinson made his debut with the Brooklyn Dodgers. Not since Moses Fleetwood Walker played for the Toledo Blue Stockings in 1884 had a Black player suited up for a team in the major leagues. After Walker, the unspoken rule was set in place that baseball became a segregated sport. What Robinson accomplished in 1947 is remarkable on so many different levels and transcends the game of baseball.

Robinson made his debut with the Dodgers at Ebbets Field in front of more than 26,000 fans. After that, wherever he would go throughout the season, many of the ballparks would sell out. Despite the harassment from fans and opposing teams, Robinson's first year was a success as he won the Rookie of the Year Award. He would have a Hall of Fame career while spending ten seasons with the Dodgers. He retired after the 1956 season and became an activist for civil rights. In my humble opinion, Robinson and Babe Ruth are the two players who did the most for baseball. And Robinson's debut on Opening Day in 1947 had to be one of the most impactful events in Major League Baseball's history.

Ian and I had tickets for the Phillies opening day on April 2, 2020, when life went off the rails. The COVID-19 situation forever changed life as we know it. What do you do when life is turned upside down? It is a true test of how a person will respond during times of crisis. In the beginning, no one in our government seemed to grasp the deadliness of the coronavirus. Was it for real? Was it a hoax? I did not know what to believe. I did not buy into any of the conspiracy theories. I just thought the United States would take the lead on finding a solution. Like the rest of the world, we waited it out and tried to stay positive. As things fall apart, we pick up the pieces as best we can.

At first, the NBA suspended its season. The NHL soon followed. The NCAA canceled its spring sports schedule. No March Madness! Spring training for baseball was put on hold in Mid-March. The Kentucky Derby and mint juleps were put on ice. Even the 2020 Summer Olympics were postponed a year. My son's Little League season was halted by the middle of March. The coach advised us we could not practice as a team. This was something bigger than sports. It was unsettling, to say the least. I missed baseball and, like everyone else, wanted life to return to a sense of normalcy. We held our collective breath.

Having no baseball was a true shock to the system. It is not just the game itself; it is the traditions and sharing of opinions and experiences of our favorite teams. I missed listening to the game on the radio. After work, I often sit in the backyard, have a beer or two and listen to Larry Andersen and Scott Franzke call the Phillies game. Andersen and Franzke are like two familiar friends who I have known for years. Even going to Ian's Little League games was a routine that stopped due to the COVID-19 situation. I did not realize how much joy it is to watch the kids play, talk with the other parents, and just be outside.

It was in the best interest of Commissioner Rob Manfred to pull the plug on baseball during spring training. He had little choice in the matter. Reading about the developing story, I felt bad for the minor league players. Players such as Mike Trout or Mookie Betts can exist financially without the game; however, minor league players are not guaranteed a salary. These players were sent home with little money in their pocket. Minor league players have many similarities to the waitresses at the Waffle House. Playing in A or AA-affiliated baseball is a lot of work with little pay and not much glory. Whether navigating several tables during a rush or diving for a ground ball, both a minor league ballplayer or Waffle House waitress maneuver with a certain amount of hustle mixed with grace and dexterity.

Not only were the players affected but also the concession workers at the ballparks, parking attendants, ushers, broadcasters, and front office staff. On top of these workers, bars, restaurants, and many secondary mom and pop businesses had to shut down. There are so many secondary jobs connected to the world of sports. When we go to a baseball game, it is hard to fathom the hard work behind the scenes.

This was not the first time of no baseball in recent memory. Major League Baseball season came to a halt during the 1994 season due to the strike. For me, that was different. People became outraged at both the players and the owners. Fans were upset, and attendance would dip when baseball finally returned in 1995. Many fans showed their displeasure by throwing things onto the field. Many just stayed away. It took steroid-induced home runs for the buzz and excitement to welcome back baseball. With the 2020 season suspended, it was more of a mixture of the fear of the unknown. All the news focused on the coronavirus. There was nothing to take one's mind off the dire circumstances.

During WW II, President Franklin D. Roosevelt wrote his famous "Green Light Letter" to keep baseball going during the war. Roosevelt's letter to Commissioner Kenesaw Mountain Landis was written on January 15, 1942. The president felt the American public "ought to have a chance at recreation" during these challenging times. Everyone stepped up to the plate. Many MLB players did serve time in the military, including Bob Feller, Joe DiMaggio, Hank Greenberg, and Ted Williams. Despite many of its star players serving overseas, baseball continued for the American public.

Finally, after arguing back and forth between the owners and the players, Major League Baseball agreed to a 60-game season starting on July 23, 2020. The games would be played in front of no fans. The first game to kick off the season would feature the New York Yankees versus the Washington Nationals. Commissioner Rob Manfred implemented the conditions to the shortened season, and the players agreed to the terms. Baseball was officially back.

The 60-game season raised some questions. Would the winner of the World Series feel like it was a true championship? The National League agreed to the DH for the 2020 season. Would this become something accepted down the road? If a batter hits over .400, would this be comparable to what Ted Williams accomplished in 1941? Would some teams have a greater advantage by playing such a short season? All these questions were valid. The most important aspect, though, was that baseball would be played during the summer once again.

With the much shorter season, MLB installed several rule changes for the year. The biggest change was the introduction of the designated hitter (DH) in the National League. This is something baseball has been talking about since Ron Blomberg of the New York Yankees came to the plate as the DH back in 1973. This rule should be universal for both leagues. Either the American League should make pitchers hit, or the National League should install the DH moving forward. The different set of rules creates an unfair advantage for the American League.

The second biggest rule change is the placement of a runner on second base when the game goes to extra innings. To help move the game along, the team at the plate will have a man on second starting in the 10th inning. Major League Baseball does not want games to drag on for 16 or 17 innings. This rule change is a bit much. One can understand with the shortened Spring Training 2.0 that players had less time to prepare for the season; however, this alters the game too much, in my humble opinion.

Some of the other rule changes for the 2020 season include pitchers being able to use a "wet rag" for their fingers. This is to eliminate licking one's fingers before gripping the ball. Relief pitchers also must face a three-batter minimum after being brought into the game. Each team was permitted to have a 60-man player pool for the season. Teams also could start the season with a 30-player roster. Due to the pandemic, players were instructed not to high-five, fist-bump, spit, hug, or basically do anything that may spread germs. Unlike the NHL or NBA, Major League Baseball chose not to play the season in a "bubble." The MLB players were free to come and go during the season.

What is so special about opening day?

Everything. Every team and every player has a fresh start. Despite the rule changes, delayed start of the season, and only playing 60 games, Major League Baseball returned for the 2020 season on July 23rd. With no crowds in the ballparks, the game felt a little different. This has been a difficult year in so many ways. The country has seen a pandemic kill more than 150,000 people, our economy slid into a recession, social protests took to our cities, people seemed angry, outraged, confused, and at a loss. On a personal level, the status of my marriage is unclear. I do not like fighting with people. Negative energy wears on a person. I do not know what tomorrow will bring. I simply try to find some brief moments of joy each day.

The Phillies and most Major League Baseball teams, restarted their spring training on Friday, July 3, 2020. Clubs settled on using their home ballparks as their Spring Training 2.0 sites. Citizens Bank Park would be the site for most of the workouts. The Phillies also chose to utilize nearby FDR Park, which was across the street from the ballpark. This way, the organization could split up the players and practice social distancing. The practices were closed to the public. Fans could not go inside Citizens Bank Park. However, FDR Park is a public park.

Ian and I decided to make the trip to FDR Park on July 4th to see if we could watch some of the practice. We both missed baseball and thought it would be fun. Since it was Independence Day, families were celebrating all through the park with barbeques and music. FDR Park is several acres, so we drove around until we found the baseball fields. Surrounded by fencing and tucked in the shadow of I-95, a few of the Phillies pitchers were taking infield practice.

Despite the heat, Ian and I watched them practice for about an hour. Signs were posted along with the fencing with instructions that the players could not interact with the fans. Only a handful of fans were watching the practice. A few of the Phillies employees walked around to keep an eye on the situation. Several reports noted that players throughout the league were testing positive for the virus. It only made sense to take precautions. Despite the rise of coronavirus cases throughout the United States and little action from the White House to address the issue, it felt good to watch some baseball. Maybe this was a sign that life could return to some normalcy. It had been a difficult year for everyone.

As we baked in the heat, one of the Phillies reserve pitchers took notice of Ian. We were the only fans standing along the fence near the third-base side. As the player was waiting his turn in some type of drill, he lobbed a ball over the chain-link fence. Ian grabbed the ball and said thank you to the player. It was a nice gesture for the Phillies player to take notice. I wish I knew who it was, but we were standing too far away. I was surprised more baseball fans were not at FDR Park to watch the team practice.

Small acts of kindness make all the difference in the world.

Standing at the chain-link fence with Ian, I thought back to the excitement of the start to the 2019 baseball season. Ian and I had tickets purchased Opening Day tickets and looked forward to seeing Bryce Harper in a Phillies uniform. On March 2, 2019, Harper had signed a 13-year deal to play in Philadelphia. Harper and Manny Machado were the two biggest free agents during the off-season. I was glad the Phillies signed Harper rather than Machado. Our fan base did not need just a great player, but one who brought energy to the ballpark. The Philadelphia sports talk radio stations finally talked about baseball rather than the Eagles or Sixers. For the first time in many years, Philadelphia fans were excited about baseball again.

If this were a normal year, Ian and I would have attended the home opener for the Phillies back in April at Citizens Bank Park. The New York Yankees and the Washington Nationals kicked off the season opener on July 23rd for the 2020 season. It made sense for these two teams to start the season. The Nationals were the World Series Champions, and the Yankees represent the classic American baseball team. These two teams have some of the biggest stars in the game. As much as I dislike the Yankees, it is hard to argue against 27 championships. The Phillies lost their first game on July 24th against the Miami Marlins. It is a baseball tradition for Philadelphia to lose on their Opening Day. With everything taking place in the world, the outcome of the game did not even matter. It was just nice to see the return of baseball.

Although fans were not permitted in the different ballparks, Philadelphia fans came up with a unique approach to cheering on the Phillies. An informal group called The Phandemic Krew started meeting outside Citizens Bank Park. It was started by two big Phillies fans named Oscar and Brett. With ladders leaning up against the fence, fans could catch a glimpse of the action inside the ballpark. Slowly, the crowd started to increase after each game. Armed with air horns and cowbells, The Phandemic Krew made its presence heard during home Phillies games. They became something of local celebrities. Oscar and Brett even had a bobblehead made of The Phandemic Krew.

Ian and I met up with friends for a Sunday doubleheader. On the afternoon we went, a fluid crowd between 50 to 100 people congregated on the sidewalk. Several ladders were leaning against the fence with fans trying to watch some of the game. One of the organizers had the radio on so everyone could listen to the game. It was like tailgating while the game was being played inside the ballpark.

"Do you want to climb the ladder?"

"Sure," Ian replied before making his way up. It was nice that someone offered to let him go up. It was still difficult to see the game, but it was better than nothing. We missed not being able to go inside to watch some baseball. Personally, I missed not going to Opening Day earlier this year. I am hoping that life will return to a more normal atmosphere in 2021. As I write these words, I cannot say I am filled with much optimism.

Looking back on Opening Day from March 28, 2019:

Ian and I arrived at the ballpark early. Our tickets were in Section 422. Although not exactly a row behind home plate, we were in the ballpark. The start time was 3:05 P.M. The Phillies were scheduled to play the Atlanta Braves. Ian was happy I took him out of school early. It made it even more special. We want to take in all the sights, sounds, smells, and get a feel for the excitement. Citizens Bank Park has an open feel to it. The Philadelphia Skyline can be seen off in the distance. From almost any location inside the ballpark, fans can look over to catch a glimpse of the field. The game is a sellout, and people have started tailgating early. The parking lot is a sea of red and white. Everyone is in their favorite Phillies gear. Although there is a chill in the air, the sun is shining brightly.

The crowd gets a little restless as the players are introduced one by one. The team added some exciting players in the off-season, including Andrew McCutchen, J.T. Realmuto, and Jean Segura. The fans are optimistic for the first time in a few years. Philadelphia has not been competitive since 2011. It was one specific player though everyone wanted to see make his debut. Before Phillies public address announcer Dan Baker calls out Bryce Harper's name, the entire ballpark is on its feet. Wearing green Phillie Phanatic-inspired cleats to go with his Phillies red pinstripes, Harper races out to a thunderous ovation. An enormous American flag stretches across the field. Everyone can feel the electricity. Ian and I are standing and cheering along with the 43,000 other fans. Philadelphia landed the biggest superstar in baseball in the off-season. Baseball was exciting again.

Every player has a blank slate on opening day. Will this be a breakout year? Will our team still be playing meaningful baseball in September and October? Will Bryce Harper bring the Phillies its third World Series Championship? Despite being founded in 1883, the Phillies have only won it all only twice. That is the same number of championships won by the Miami Marlins. The Phanatic rallies the crowd. The grass looks extra green, and despite the cool weather, spring is here. It is a long season, but the fans hopeful. My son and I stand along with everyone else in the ballpark. Aaron Nola takes the mound for the Phillies. The catcher flashes his signs. The batter digs into the batter's box.

The crowd waits in anticipation.

The start of a new season is upon us.

AFTERWORD

The 2020 baseball season was completed despite the pandemic, with the Los Angeles Dodgers winning the World Series on October 27, 2020. It was truly a season like no other in the history of baseball. Unfortunately, the year was a difficult one for the sport as several legendary people close to the game passed away. Dick Allen, Lou Brock, Bob Gibson, Whitey Ford, Phil Niekro, and Tom Seaver died in 2020. As a Phillies fan, I am not old enough to have watched Allen hit some of his legendary moonshots for the team at Connie Mack Stadium.

The start of 2021 saw the passing of legendary Dodgers Tommy Lasorda. One of my favorite Lasorda moments is when he beat up the Phillie Phanatic at Veterans Stadium on August 28, 1988. Lasorda did not take too kindly of the Phanatic making fun of his beloved Dodgers. It was a classic moment for the legendary Dodgers manager. Unfortunately, a few weeks after Lasorda's passing, we lost another baseball legend.

Hank Aaron passed away on January 22, 2021. Most known for passing Babe Ruth on the all-time home run list, Aaron was a great all-around ballplayer. He received death threats and hate mail while chasing Ruth's home run record. In addition to his 755 home runs, Aaron also amassed 3,771 hits over his 23-year career. He was a tremendous ambassador for baseball and civil rights, treating people with kindness, and getting young people involved in the game. He grew up poor in Mobile, Alabama but overcame all obstacles to achieve baseball greatness. His Major League Baseball career stretched from 1954 to 1976. Somewhat forgotten is Aaron also played for the Indianapolis Clowns in the Negro American League in 1952. He was paid $200 per month to play for the Clowns. The past is not so long ago. I wish I could have seen Aaron play baseball in person.

On a personal level, I am still trying to sort things out. It was not an easy decision, but Sara and I decided to file for divorce. With three kids and after more than 20 years together, I am not sure what the future holds. Relationships are always a challenge. Sara is a good person. Our marriage just did not work out in the end. My son Ian was able to play fall baseball in 2020 with certain restrictions in place due to COVID-19. He had to have his temperature checked before games. All the kids were required to wear face coverings while in the dugout. It was nice, though, just to see the kids able to play baseball again. The spring 2021 Little League season was given the green light. Also, the Phillies announced a limited number of fans could watch games at Citizens Bank Ballpark for the 2021 season. So life is returning to normal.

The year 2020 was difficult for everyone. With the virus, political division, protests, an uneven economy, and everything else, it was hard to find something positive. However, I will never again take for granted the simple joy of sitting at Citizens Bank Park with my family and enjoying a ballgame. Thank you for taking the time to read my book.

BIBLIOGRAPHY

BOOKS

Ackerman, M. (2010). *Curveball: The Remarkable Story of Toni Stone, the First Woman to Play Professional Baseball in the Negro League.* Chicago, IL: Lawrence Hill Books.

Anonymous. (2007, March 29). Disgraced Little Leaguer Almonte signs a minor-league deal with Southern Illinois Miners. *National News,* S7.

Associated Press. (1987, September 2). Potato scheme is half-baked. *The Washington Post,* B4.

Associated Press. (2019, August 23). Put me in coach: Youth baseball participation is on the rise. *USA Today,* retrieved from https://www.com/story /sports/mlb/2019/08/23/put-me-in-coach-youth-baseball-participation -on-the-rise/40002827.

ASPJ Staff. (2003). The Wright brothers. *Air & Space Power Journal,* Winter 2003, Vol. 17 (4), 30

Breen, M. (2020, July 11). Phil' Irish Mike Ryan dies. *The Philadelphia Inquirer,* C4.

Breen, M. (2021, January 23). Hank Aaron: He knocked racism out of the ballpark. *The Philadelphia Inquirer,* A1–A2.

Cacciola, S. (2013, July 18). Rich man frayed city. *The New York Times,* B11.

Chavets, Z. (2009). *Cooperstown Confidential.* New York, NY: Bloomsbury.

Colbert, J. (2010). *Insider's Guide to Baltimore.* Guilford, CT: Morris Book Publishing.

Coyle, J. (1986, November 8). Dunes of North Carolina mark site of Wright brothers 1st flight in 1903. *The Toronto Star,* H23.

Debnam, B. (1987, June 7). Father's Day History. *The Washington Post,* MP2.

Dillow, C. (2013). Comfort food: How Waffle House became a disaster indicator for FEMA. *Popular Science,* Vol. 283(5), 27-28.

Fallin, A. and Stanton, A. (2015). Tobacco-control policies in tobacco-growing states: Where tobacco was king. *The Milbank Quarterly,* Vol. 93 (2), 319–358.

Fleitz, D. (2001). *Shoeless: The Life and Times of Joe Jackson.* Jefferson, NC: McFarland & Company.

Fitzpatrick, F. (2019, July 27). A summer tradition in decline. *The Philadelphia Inquirer,* C1–C2.

Fitzpatrick, F. (2020, May 3). No minor loss. *The Philadelphia Inquirer,* C1–C2.

Giles, B. (2007). *Pouring Six Beers at a Time: And Other Stories from a Lifetime of Baseball.* Chicago, IL: Triumph Books.

Hamilton, J. (2010). *Beyond Belief: Finding the Strength to Come Back.* New York, NY: Faith Words.

Hummer, S. (2016, July 5). The fourth and fort perfect for baseball. *The Atlantic-Journal Constitution,* C2.

Kinkaid, K. (2020, August 28). Today in Sports History: Tommy Lasorda vs. The Phillie Phanatic. *Crossing Broad.* https://www.crossingbroad.com/2020/08/today-in-sports-history-tommy-lasorda-vs-the-phillie-phanatic.html

Leavy, J. (2018). *The Big Fella: Babe Ruth and the World He Created.* New York, NY: HarperCollins.

Moore, A. (2013). Rebranding in Reading: How an ostrich shook up 'Baseball Town.' *Public Relations Tactics,* Vol. 20(3), 17.

Nelson, C. (2014, May 22). Obama tries out Babe Ruth's bat, Joe DiMaggio's glove. *Dow Jones Newswires.*

Newton, J. (1980). William Judy Johnson: Delaware's folk hero of the diamond. *Negro History Bulletin,* Vol. 43(4), 91 & 94.

Nightengale, B. (2011, September 15). Varitek basks in the twilight. *USA Today,* C1.

Pace, L. (1988, June 1). Durham is bullish on baseball. *Business-North Carolina,* Pg. 42, v8, n6, Section 1.

Perry, T. (2004). *Textile League Baseball: South Carolina's Mill Teams, 1880–1955.* Jefferson, NC: McFarland &Company.

Sanchez, R. (2020). Minor leagues, major changes. *Sports Illustrated,* Vol. 131 (6), 32–41.

Siegel, A. (2018, July 14). *Unrequited love story: 'Bull Durham' at 30.* The Ringer. https://www.theringer.com/movies/2018/6/14/17451268/bull-durham-30-anniversary-kevin-costner-ron-shelton-susan-sarandon

Smith, B. (2020, February 1) *Former Phillies player Steve Jeltz emphasizes the positive at Berks clinic.* Reading Eagle. https://www.readingeagle.com/sports/former-phillies-player-steve-jeltz-emphasizes-the-positive-at-berks-clinic/article_5c78ff10-4558-11ea-8d9d-2b0d4c4b0d3c.html

Sorvino. C. (2020, March 29). *Crippled by coronavirus, Waffle House faces a harsh reality: 'We've never seen anything like this.'* Forbes website. https://www.forbes.com/sites/chloesorvino/2020/03/29/crippled-by-coronavirus-waffle-house-faces-a-harsh-reality-weve-never-seen-anything-like-this/#272085a732c5

Tagami, T. (2010, September 18). Kid Rock, entourage lose lawsuit, $40,000. *The Atlanta-Journal Constitution*, B5.

Vaught, D. (2011). From tobacco patch to pitcher's mound: Gaylord Perry, the spitter, and farm life in Eastern North Carolina. *Journal of Southern History*, Vol. 77, (4), 865–894.

WEBSITES

https://axewomen.com
https://www.baseball-almanac.com
https://baseballhall.org
https://www.baseballpilgrimages.com
https://www.baseball-reference.com
https://www.berkshistory.org
https://www.coastalplain.com
https://www.darenc.com
http://www.desports.org
https://www.espn.com
https://www.findlaymarketparade.com
https://hamptonpirates.com/sports/softball/roster
https://www.imdb.com
https://www.legion.org
https://www.littleleague.org
https://www.milb.com/carolina-league
https://www.milb.com/clinton
https://www.milb.com/pensacola
https://www.milb.com/reading
https://www.milb.com/rocky-mountain
https://www.milb.com/williamsport
https://www.milb.com/wilmington
https://www.mlb.com/phillies
https://www.mlb.com/reds
http://ncbaseballmuseum.com

https://nlbm.com
http://www.nlbpa.com
https://www.nps.gov/articles/wright-brothers.htm
https://www.nps.gov/wrbr
https://www.outerbanks.com
https://www.playball.org
http://pointstreaksites.com/view/alaskabaseballleague
https://www.ourstate.com
https://www.readingpa.gov
https://sabr.org
https://www.sheetz.com/
https://www.shoelessjoejackson.org
http://sussexcountyminers.com
http://tidewatersummerleague.com
https://www.wafflehouse.com/
https://visitlycomingcounty.com
https://www.yardbarker.com

ABOUT THE AUTHOR

JASON LOVE lives in New Jersey. He has a history degree from West Chester University in Pennsylvania. Throughout the year, he gives lectures on baseball at local libraries and for the Rutgers University Osher Lifelong Learning Institute (OLLI-RU). His career batting average in Little League was .210 with zero home runs.

Made in the USA
Middletown, DE
13 October 2021